THE NEW
RULES
OF
MANAGEMENT

THE NEW
RULES
OF
MANAGEMENT

**How to Revolutionise
Productivity, Innovation and Engagement
by Implementing Projects That Matter**

PETER COOK

WILEY

First published in 2013 by John Wiley & Sons Australia, Ltd

42 McDougall St, Milton Qld 4064

Office also in Melbourne

Typeset in ITC Berkeley Oldstyle Std Book 11.5/13

© Peter Cook Enterprises Pty Ltd

The moral rights of the author have been asserted

National Library of Australia Cataloguing-in-Publication data:

Author:	Cook, Peter.
Title:	The new rules of management: how to revolutionise productivity, innovation and engagement by implementing projects that matter / Peter Cook.
ISBN:	9781118606261 (pbk.)
Notes:	Includes index.
Subjects:	Project management
Dewey Number:	658.404

Cover design by Michael Freeland

Internal illustrations and author photograph by Michael Fink

Printed in Singapore by C.O.S. Printers Pte Ltd

10 9 8 7 6 5 4 3 2 1

Disclaimer

Contents

About the author

Peter Cook is passionate about helping people and organisations implement the important stuff. He is a master business coach, mentor, serial entrepreneur, author, and a warm and engaging presenter.

He has more than 15 years experience as a consultant and business coach, working with hundreds of businesses from one-man start-ups to some of the biggest companies in the world. Peter runs programs across Australia, New Zealand, Asia and the United States to help thought leaders and organisations implement the projects that matter.

Peter is a smart cookie. He holds a Masters of Business in Organisational Change, a Bachelor of Science in Advanced Physics and Bachelor of Laws with Honours.

He is happily married to his gorgeous wife, Trish, and, at the time of publishing, he and Trish had just welcomed their first daughter, Scarlett, into the family. The final manuscript of this book was due the same week as the baby. If these two projects weren't challenging enough, that week Peter and Trish also moved into their new house, which they had rebuilt in less than two months. When it comes to implementation, Pete clearly practises what he preaches!

Peter believes strongly in giving back to the community. He is the president of Buoyancy, a not-for-profit drug and alcohol counselling service, and is leading a team that has raised $300 000 over five years to end hunger for a group of villages in

Senegal, West Africa. He has a second dan black belt in aikido (so don't mess with him!), and is an Olympic-level downhill skier trapped in the body of an average skier.

After a decade of small business coaching, he now focuses on mentoring other thought leaders, whether they be consultants going it alone or leaders within larger organisations. In his spare time he plays significant roles in a couple of start-ups, writes the odd book, speaks about implementation and consults to organisations on their projects that matter.

You can find out what Pete is currently up to and get in touch at www.petercook.com.

Acknowledgements

First, of course, to my beautiful wife, Trish. Thanks for sharing so many amazing projects with me, and creating a life together where anything is possible. Everything is better because of you. Scarlett, my baby daughter, thanks for waiting until I got this book finished before showing up.

To my father Nev: thanks for fighting to make this book the best it could be. For thinking critically about every model and every big idea down to every comma and full stop. As always, you make my writing and my thinking better.

Thanks also go to my mother, Ola, for teaching me the importance of finding the heart and beauty in everything I do, and for your complete support along my journey, through my successes and more importantly through some of my more spectacular failures.

To Cristina, my business manager, thanks for partnering me tirelessly in so many amazing projects in our business, for your commitment to excellence in everything we do, and your willingness to keep being thrown in the deep end with every new project we launch.

Matt Church—my mentor, partner and friend, and the best implementer I know—this (and many other things in my life) wouldn't have happened without you.

Michael Fink, my best mate and designer extraordinaire, thanks for trying to make me look good with everything that has my name on it, for caring more than me about the importance of good design, teaching me to be annoyed by bad kerning and learning about typesetting just for this project.

Thanks to Jason Fox, Michael Henderson, Derek Sivers and Josh Kaufman. Thanks for your thought leadership, for speaking to me about your areas of expertise and contributing to the book.

And finally thanks to Lucy, Alice, Elizabeth, Meryl, Keira, Gretta, Katie and the whole team at Wiley for making this book one of their projects that matter, and for fighting just as hard as me to make it the best book it could possibly be.

Gratitude, love and respect to you all.

Introduction

What got you here won't get you there.

Marshall Goldsmith, author and executive coach

The first working title for this book was *The End of Management*, but we eventually decided that that was being a bit too dramatic, and not entirely accurate. But one thing I am certain of is that the way we have managed our organisations, our teams and even our lives in the past isn't cutting it any more. The things that have made us successful in the past are insufficient for the present and the future. Or, as Albert Einstein said, 'The problems that exist in the world today cannot be solved by the level of thinking that created them'.

The game of management has changed, and if we want to win the new game, we need to understand the new rules.

A number of frustrations led me to write this book. The first is seeing, time and again, organisations letting great ideas wither on the vine.

I do a lot of innovation training and consulting to big companies in Australia and around the world. Often I am brought in to help an organisation come up with innovative solutions to a challenge they are facing, or an opportunity that has presented itself. Usually I will spend a day or two facilitating a process of ideation with key staff from the company. We'll use a number of different processes to come up with creative ideas. It's quite common for me to go home at the end of the day being really impressed by the calibre of thinking from the people I have worked with, and the strength of the ideas that they have come up with.

Unfortunately, there's another part of that tale that is all too common. Six months later I will check in to see how things are going, only to find nothing has been done. 'Business as usual' took over, and everyone got too busy doing what they were already doing to execute any of their great ideas. Which means the entire process was a waste of time and money—a great idea not executed is worse than there being no idea in the first place. And so I have realised that a process to come up with great ideas is insufficient: we need to know how to implement those ideas too.

I get even more frustrated when I see teams that are using only a fraction of their potential. Teams that operate in a Dilbert-like environment, where bureaucracy trumps achievement, and work becomes soul destroying. Work cultures that don't give people the opportunity to do their best work, and jobs where people end up surviving until the weekend rather than doing something that matters, that stretches them and that they could be proud of. I think it is criminal to take intelligent, passionate, creative, switched-on people, and manage them like cogs in a machine.

My final frustration is at an individual level when I experience wasted talent and lost opportunity. We live in an age of possibility, where in the developed world we have an infinite number of choices, and opportunities like never before to design our lives to go however we want. Yet for many of us it seems this freedom is crippling. We don't come close to reaching our potential, and end up not being as productive as we could be or as successful as we envisage, and ultimately we remain unfulfilled.

For almost 20 years I have been working as a consultant and a business coach, and running my own businesses. Over that time I have had the privilege to work with lots of great leaders, amazing teams and some of the biggest and most successful organisations in the world. And through that time I have been a keen student of success: what does it take to succeed? Why do some organisations succeed where others fail? Why do some teams rock, while others suck? And why are some people successful and fulfilled, while others are unproductive, frustrated and dissatisfied?

This book is an attempt to take what I have learned from these great organisations and successful people and see what they have in common. It isn't great products, charismatic leadership, intelligence, resources, or any of the things we normally associate with success. The one critical element to success is the intent, willingness and ability to implement projects that matter. This applies in our organisations, our teams, and in our lives.

I believe there is an implementation imperative for every one of us. We each have a limited window, and if we want to be successful and leave a legacy, we need to implement much, much more. We need to shift our focus to creating and executing the projects that matter, in our lives as well as at work.

Likewise, the creation and execution of projects that matter is what will transform teams from being a drain on our spirits to experiences of being stretched and growing, and making a difference in the world. A change from teams of people going through the motions, to teams comprising motivated, engaged, switched-on people performing at their peak.

At an organisational level the need to implement is even more stark. Put simply, managing just your existing business, even managing it well, could put you out of business. Organisations need to implement projects that create growth on all levels, or face extinction at the hands of the next disruptive technology in their industry.

My hope is that you use the concepts and the models in this book, not to make an incremental improvement, not to evolve a bit more, but to revolutionise the way you live and work.

Chapter 1

IMPLEMENTATION
—————— IN A ——————
NUTSHELL

I want to know what you will do about it. I do not want to know what you hope for. I want to know what you will work for. I do not want your sympathy for the needs of humanity. I want your muscle. As the wagon driver said when they came to a long, hard hill, 'Them that's going on with us, get out and push. Them that ain't, get out of the way.'

Robert Fulghum, author of *All I Really Need to Know I Learned in Kindergarten*

Traditional management practices focus on managing systems and responses, increasing efficiency, and creating more profit in the short term—what we call 'left of the line' activities.

Management in the 21st century requires much more than this. The new rules of management demand a relentless focus on implementation (creation and execution of projects). In other words, the actions that live to the right of the line. I believe implementing projects that matter is the most important thing we do personally, in our teams and in our organisations.

Wherever we look—and we will be looking in lots of places—we find that implementing important projects and doing work that matters is the key to productivity, fulfilment, engagement, innovation and success.

There is no magic bullet that managers can call on to grow profits, drive creativity, increase performance, lift engagement—or even give us world peace. But if there were, it would be implementing projects that matter.

So that we are on the same page, a project is very basically a significant outcome delivered by a specific time. Having a book published by the end of the year is a project—doing more writing isn't a project. Running the City to Surf this year without walking at all is a project. Joining a gym isn't. Increasing sales by 15 per cent this quarter is a project. Growing the business isn't.

This book is divided into three domains: personal, team and organisation. Let's look at why managers face an implementation imperative in each of them.

Personal

Your hardware—your neurology, neural pathways, biology, biochemistry and physique—has evolved over hundreds of thousands of years. As a species, features that have enhanced our chances of survival have been selected, while features that diminished our chances of survival have been eliminated. Now bear with me while we do a little time travel into our deep past.

In round numbers, we have been hunter-gatherers for many hundreds of thousands of years. During that time, evolution honed our skills as hunter-gatherers so we could survive in the world as it was then. New discoveries show we actually evolved in fits and starts, and it was a 200 000-year period of violent, unpredictable climate change that spurred one of the biggest leaps in our evolution—the leap that actually created what we would recognise as modern-day humans.

About 12 000 years ago people started farming, so we have been farmers rather than hunter-gatherers for only a fraction of the time humans have been around. The industrial revolution started more than 250 years ago, and the information age has been with us for a bit more than a generation—I first used email about 25 years ago.

For most of our evolution the name of the game has been survival. Your hardware was designed so you could survive as a hunter-gatherer in Africa. Your fight-or-flight response is state of the art for that purpose. If a lion crosses your path, a whole bunch of things happen that will help you survive, without you having to think about it. Your senses send signals to the parietal and occipital lobes of the brain along the brain stem, and the amygdala—a tiny region at the top of the brain stem—sends a quick message to the frontal lobe. If your body doesn't get an immediate instruction telling it how to respond, the hypothalamus of the brain takes control and begins a cascade of hormones that, among other things, surges hydrocortisone into your bloodstream to increase blood supply to your major muscles, allowing you to either stand and fight, or run for your life. At the same time, your digestion shuts down, and your immune system is suppressed, so you do not waste any energy on non-essential activities. Your heart rate increases, as adrenaline is released into the blood stream. All of this gives you the best possible chance to survive an imminent threat.

If you're reading this book, your survival is pretty much taken care of. You're not going to get eaten by a lion any time soon. You are going to have a roof over your head, clothes on your back and food in your belly for the rest of your life. The bottom rung of Maslow's hierarchy of needs is all good.

The game has changed. Now it's all about thriving in the information age, not surviving in the Stone Age. The game of thriving in the information age is won by implementing the projects that matter, but you're playing this new game with outdated hardware.

Imagine if you were designed to be great at implementing important projects, and your project was to write a book. When you sat down to start work, you'd get a little dopamine hit (the feel-good drug in your brain), making you feel optimistic and helping you overcome any resistance to starting difficult work. When you hit a roadblock along the way, all sorts of things could kick in to help you overcome it — you would feel more awake, alert, focused, confident and committed (rather than tired, overwhelmed or inadequate, and thinking that anything would be better than this).

Instead you are using hardware that wasn't designed for this. That's fine. It can get the job done but there are a few things that we can do that will make life much easier. The first tip is simply to recognise that while your hardware is absolutely state of the art when it comes to dealing with a lion crossing your path, it's pretty inadequate for what you are asking of it now. That's about your hardware, not about you. You will struggle, and that's to be expected. Go easy on yourself.

The second thing to do is install some hacks and some workarounds that will improve things. And that's what the rest of this book will help you with.

The key to personal success and fulfilment

I don't think the key to being successful in your business or career, your relationships, your health, your finances, or anything else for that matter, is being intelligent, or well resourced or even well connected—although these things all help. I think the single most important factor in your success is your ability to implement significant projects.

The problem is, we are told that success is about character. It's about integrity. It's about attitude. It's about discipline. But plenty of people have all of these attributes and still don't achieve wild success.

It's still true that we are all 100 per cent responsible for our own success — but it's just not in the way you think. What if there were some shortcuts to success you weren't aware of? What if these shortcuts allowed you to borrow enough discipline, integrity and winning attitude to achieve your goals? Could it be possible that, where you haven't succeeded, it's because you didn't create the right context, or put together the right support? In other words, because you didn't structure your success properly?

Every action we take has long-term and short-term implications. In the short term, an action will give us pleasure or pain. In the long term, an action will be either beneficial or detrimental.

As you can see in the fulfilment model shown in figure 1.1 (overleaf), at the bottom level are the stupid things we do. These are the things that give us short-term pain and are detrimental in the long term. For example, for me playing golf is plain stupid. It generally takes me about five years to forget how bad I am at golf. So even though for the previous four years I have knocked back every invitation to play golf, in the fifth year, for some strange reason, I will think it's a good idea. I will picture the ball sailing down the middle of the fairway and imagine the satisfaction I'll feel. Of course that illusion is shattered at the first tee, and I'm in for a frustrating afternoon with the probability of needing therapy to rebuild my damaged psyche. There are things we all do which, however you look at it, are just plain stupid.

Figure 1.1: fulfilment model

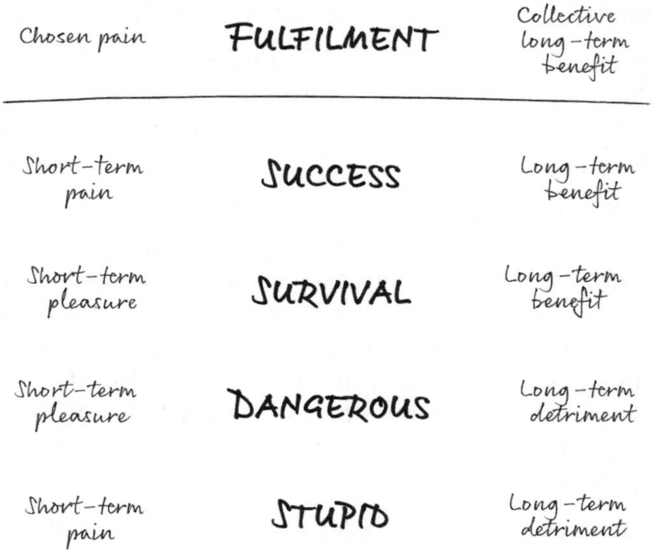

Chosen pain	FULFILMENT	Collective long—term benefit
Short-term pain	SUCCESS	Long-term benefit
Short-term pleasure	SURVIVAL	Long-term benefit
Short-term pleasure	DANGEROUS	Long-term detriment
Short-term pain	STUPID	Long-term detriment

Then there are the dangerous things we do. The things that give us short-term pleasure, but are detrimental in the longer term. Junk food is like that for me: I love the taste, enjoy eating it, but half an hour later I regret it. The reason these things are dangerous is that we are set up to do things that give us pleasure or take us away from pain. And historically it was rarely a problem.

Our ancestors didn't have the option of thinking: 'For dinner tonight, shall we spend a day hunting and gathering, get in a good amount of exercise, breathe fresh air, get some sunshine, and then have a meal of organic lean meat, fresh herbs and vegetables? Nah, stuff it. Let's order a pizza, get some DVDs and drink some beer.'

But now we do have that option, and so the very thing we have evolved to do (take actions that give us immediate pleasure or take away pain) can get us into trouble. We see the evidence of this every day, and experience it in our own lives.

The survival category in the fulfilment model (see figure 1.1) includes the things that cause us pleasure in the short term and are beneficial in the long term. For example eating when you're hungry, putting on clothes when you're cold or sleeping when you're tired. We have evolved to do all these things, because they have helped us survive. These things are easy.

The problem for us today is that we don't need to learn how to implement to survive, but we do need to learn how to implement to thrive. Today, success comes from being able to take actions that give us short-term pain but are beneficial in the long term. The ability to defer gratification is what it takes to achieve our higher goals and aspirations, like fulfilment.

Fulfilment transcends stupidity, danger, survival and even success. Here we choose the short-term discomfort, so we don't suffer long-term pain. At the level of fulfilment, we no longer have the experience of it being painful, even if we are deferring gratification.

Implementation is the key to the top two categories in the fulfilment model—success and fulfilment. The success of your life comes down to the important projects you have implemented. If you review your last 90 days and ask the question 'How successful were they?' the answer will come down to the projects you implemented.

Even more tellingly, if you imagine reviewing your whole life while sitting on your rocking chair on the porch, celebrating your 100th birthday, success will come down to the quality of your relationships of course, and to the projects that you implemented over your life.

Likewise, fulfilment comes from doing great things, contributing what we have to the world, making a difference in the lives of others: in other words, implementing projects that matter.

Before we think about creating and executing projects that matter in our teams and organisation, it is critical we start in our own backyard. Success as a manager can't simply exist in the office. If projects matter, they matter everywhere. So we look first at the personal domain — our health, our money, our family, our fitness, our relationships. Implementing projects that matter here will strengthen our resolve to do so in our teams and our organisations. And we will have integrity — we won't be telling our people to do as we say, but not as we do.

Team

Many of us spend most of our waking hours at work, and working in teams. This is an incredible responsibility for anybody who is a manager, including, as it does, responsibility for the output of the team and the results that are produced. However, I believe there is an even greater responsibility for the input — the team members who show up and give their life force to their work.

When I teach people about how to think about money, and specifically about spending consciously, I borrow a concept from *Your Money or Your Life* (a great book by Vicki Robin and Joe Dominguez about achieving financial independence). It's the idea that money equates to life energy. When we work we are exchanging our life energy for money, and when we spend our money we are spending our life energy. It's not the whole truth, but it's a powerful perspective that helps people become more conscious of their spending.

The people who show up to work in your team are using their life energy in service of the work of the organisation. This can either be used in service of something worthwhile, or wasted.

Waste makes me angry. I get angry when I see food in silos rotting when I know that 20 000 people die every day from hunger-related causes. I get angry when I see entire office buildings lit up at night and I know that we have a finite amount of natural resources we're burning up. But I get even angrier when I see people's spirit being wasted away.

People show up wanting to do work that matters, wanting to make a difference, wanting to be challenged, to grow, to be lit up—and yet so often the reality is the exact opposite.

I think of the gap between the reality of what teams are actually doing and their full potential as wasted possibility. That gap—that wasted possibility—is sometimes so large as to be almost criminal. I think that the ultimate measure of anyone who leads a team is how much of that potential is actually achieved.

Teams that experience Mondayitis, who call Wednesday hump day, and say 'Thank God it's Friday'—teams that survive the week and live for the weekend—could be so much more.

Of course the key to those magic teams, the teams where people are lit up, giving all of themselves and doing great work is implementation: the creation and execution of projects that matter.

This is also the key to attracting and retaining great people. Projects that matter are the new currency on a modern résumé. An old résumé listed education and responsibilities—this is what I learnt, and this is the university or college that would take me, and this is what I was accountable for. A 21st-century résumé is much more about answering the question: 'What were the great projects you were part of?' This trend is increasing, which means that to attract the best people, you need to give them the opportunity to be a part of great projects.

The reason we need to put time and energy and love into creating a culture of implementation in our teams is that it's hard to do. We are trained into an industrial revolution mentality — of quality control and wanting to manage out errors. We act as if our team is a machine, and we want to make sure all the parts work together smoothly. This kind of thinking is fine for an industrial revolution organisation. If your team is working on an assembly line putting together Model-T Fords, you don't want them creating and executing projects that matter. You want them following the system with as few errors as possible.

This is what we learned in Management 101: we learned how to create budgets, put together plans, do performance reviews and manage our teams like they were part of a system. However, if you have a team of knowledge workers in the 21st century, that isn't going to cut it any more, because, to put it quite simply, you need to lead them in the implementation of great projects. That's what the new rules of management demand, and what success in a modern team requires.

Organisation

Why did Apple win? In 2012 Apple had the highest market capitalisation (that is, value) of any public company in the world. Of course the game is still on, and five years from now the story might be very different. Whatever happens from here, there can be no argument that Apple's success has been nothing less than phenomenal.

It's not because it has great customer service. In fact it is renowned for ignoring what customers ask for, and producing what they think will rock. It's not because of clever marketing — its primary marketing strategy has been to create cool products that people love and will talk about. It's because of a single-minded focus on implementation.

Fifteen years ago, when Steve Jobs returned to Apple, he didn't try to do what they were already doing but just a little bit better. He simply decided the company would launch lots of great projects, fail most, and win big when they succeed. Jobs initially identified four distinct gaps and said, 'Let's make insanely great products to fill these gaps'. And while he might not have expressed it like this, he launched four projects that matter. And Apple has kept doing that to become the biggest music distributor in the world, the most profitable phone company in the world and the most valuable public company in the world.

Saying that Apple is all about creating and executing projects that matter wouldn't be far off. If you look at its product list it's like a ticker-tape parade of great projects: projects that started as great ideas and were implemented like crazy.

Organisations in the 19th century were characterised by industrialisation. In most domains this was the first time big organisations were being formed. People were coming together to increase efficiencies, and as a result the standard of living and the population of the planet both increased markedly.

The 20th century was all about management. Management theory evolved throughout this century from the father of scientific management, Frederick Taylor, through to Peter Drucker, inventor of 'management by objectives', and onto many others. This was when management consultants (my first job title) took off, and management gurus were born. If industrialisation was all about bringing organisations together, traditional management was about making them work better, more efficiently, more productively and with fewer errors. Put simply, management aimed to identify the core business; do it better; and do it faster.

In the 21st century, the new rules of management are all about implementation. The organisations that will survive, and thrive, are those that focus on implementing—those whose very DNA is about creating and executing projects that matter, who are all about implementing innovative projects that create new business. Apple's current success is an early indication of this trend. Improving on the core business is no longer enough.

Clayton Christensen, the Kim B. Clark Professor of Business Administration at the Harvard Business School, did some amazing research into a series of companies that went out of business when a disruptive technology came along. He wrote a book about his findings—*The Innovator's Dilemma: When New Technologies Cause Great Firms to Fail*. And his findings were startling. He concluded that these companies did not fail because of bad management, but because of good management. He found that good management practice, which focused on the core business and existing customers, actually drives the failure of successful firms when they are faced with disruptive technology. We need to move from a management paradigm to an implementation paradigm in order to survive.

Unfortunately, most organisations are still set up in an old management paradigm. We measure the wrong things. Turnover, profit, share-price—our primary measures and key performance indicators in business—generally tell us how well our core business is going. An implementation focus will hurt those numbers in the short term. Generally, investing time, money and resources into projects that matter will initially increase expenses for no immediate increase in turnover. Of course, in two years or five years or ten years, we will see the return.

An implementation strategy says: 'Let's keep doing what we're doing, because it's our core business that allows us to do new, great things. Let's also launch some magical, audacious, risky projects and expect most of them to fail.' And the ones that succeed? They are our new strategy.

How to implement projects that matter

Hopefully you're now convinced that implementation—the creation and execution of projects that matter—is important. Maybe it's the most important thing we do—and it's difficult. Personally, in our teams and in our organisations, we are just not wired for long-term projects. Fortunately, implementation is a skill that can be learnt, a muscle that can be developed. The remainder of this book is all about how to implement projects that matter. It is based upon the primary implementation model shown in figure 1.2.

Figure 1.2: primary implementation model

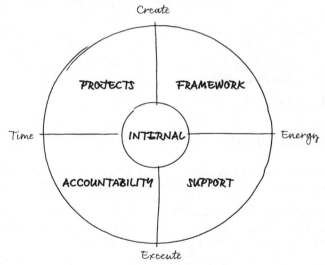

Create and execute

Every project must be created and executed, and this makes up the vertical axis of our primary implementation model in figure 1.2 (p. 13).

Stephen Covey, author of *The 7 Habits of Highly Effective People*, says that to know, but not to do, is not really to know. In other words, ideas that don't lead to action aren't really worth anything.

Inventor Thomas Edison famously quantified the distinction between creation and execution when he said that genius was 'one per cent inspiration and 99 per cent perspiration'. Edison, like this book, had a bias towards action and execution.

When we think about innovation we often make the mistake of thinking it's all about creativity. We look for creative thinkers, and innovation training is largely about how to ideate—how to come up with more ideas. However, a brilliant idea not executed is worthless, just like a great insight that doesn't lead to action makes no difference.

Implementation requires creation *and* execution.

Time and energy

The horizontal axis in figure 1.2 represents time and energy, and of course implementing anything requires both.

Implementing anything takes time, and a project is either finished on time, or it isn't. The flow of time is a critical element of both the creation and execution of projects.

A lot of headspace goes into managing time, but it is actually managing energy that is more important. One of the reasons implementing projects is difficult is that they take energy, and more often than not they require expending energy now for a reward that happens much later.

Internal and external

There are internal and external elements to implementation. The internal elements are things like mindset, character and discipline, on a personal level; and things like culture and climate, when we look at our teams and organisations. The external elements are the structures we put around ourselves.

One of the myths of implementing projects that matter is that the art of implementation is predominantly internal. If we hear a motivational speaker talk about their success, they generally list all internal reasons—mindset, character, belief, discipline, integrity, and so on. Likewise the success or failure of our teams and organisations is largely attributed to the organisational equivalent—culture. And while all these internal components are important, success or failure of major projects is influenced more by the external structures—the things we put around ourselves and our teams to implement projects.

Five elements of implementation

So, whether we are implementing projects in our personal lives, our teams or our organisations, there are five elements that we need to consider—you can see them all on the primary implementation model in figure 1.2. The first is the internal component—our mindset when we are looking at things personally, and the culture and climate of our teams and organisations. The four external elements are projects, framework, support and accountability.

Think about any long-term, meaningful goal that you have achieved, and you will find that all of these elements were present. Your mindset was aligned with the goal; you made a clear choice to go for that goal or undertake that project; and you were committed to it—not just interested in it. You had a framework and a methodology: you knew what to do (or you learnt it along the way) and you were clear about why you were doing it. You had support: there were people in your life who were on your side, and you had an accountability structure to achieve the goal.

Now think about a long-term goal that you didn't achieve. One or more of these elements would probably have been missing. Perhaps you hadn't really chosen the project; you weren't clear on the methodology (that is, you didn't know what to do); you didn't have the support (in other words, someone to be accountable to); or the right structures in place that showed you what to do when. Yet, in your mind, you were probably saying you didn't achieve the goal because you weren't good enough; you didn't have enough discipline; or you were flawed in some way. Not true! It's just that you didn't structure the project effectively.

One of the reasons the university business model is so effective is that a university or college provides all the external elements required. I completed a bachelor degree in science in advanced physics at a Melbourne university straight out of high school. I now reflect on my lectures and that whole experience in almost speechless disbelief at how inefficient the whole process was, and how I passively allowed such a monumental waste of my time.

The standard model of undergraduate university teaching is something like this:

1 Read some background material.

2 Turn up to a lecture and take notes about what the lecturer talks about.

3 Summarise your notes and complete an assignment based on the notes.

4 Go to small tutorials to discuss these notes.

5 Sit an exam to test your memory of these notes.

A few years ago I was clearing out old boxes of papers when I stumbled across a thermodynamics exam that I had aced about 15 years earlier. I'd received 94 per cent for it. I looked through the questions and found not only that I couldn't do them—I didn't even understand them. I wouldn't have known where to start.

I remember preparing for the exam for that subject. The same professor had been teaching the subject for a decade, and looking at the previous exams we realised that his questions were on about a three-year rotation. If you could answer all the questions from the last three years' exams, you were pretty safe. So that's what I did. I played the game, committed those questions to my short-term memory, and learned pretty much nothing.

So what is the attraction of university? Why is this teaching model and business model still so attractive when the field of adult learning has come so far? I could have learned much more about physics and thermodynamics by spending the same amount of time with the right books, and these days the right websites.

It's because university gives us these four structures:

1 *Projects*. All the projects are created for us. There is the three-year project called the degree, the one-year project called year one (or two, or three) and the 15-week project called a semester, or a subject. We don't need to create our own long-term projects (which we are not that good at) because it's done for us.

2 *Framework*. The context, environment and methodology are all provided. Learning thermodynamics off your own bat would be difficult—we wouldn't know how. Which are the good books to read and which aren't? How should we sequence the different topics? What exercises should

we do? How should we chunk it? The university provides the methodology to follow and the environment to show up to.

3 *Support*. At university we get the support of our friends, our tutors, our lecturers and professors and the whole university infrastructure. We don't have to tackle our education on our own. Enrolment comes with a support structure.

4 *Accountability*. There is an accountability structure outside us. There are lectures to turn up to, tutorials to attend, papers to submit and exams to sit. If we don't show up it's noticed.

Because, for an undergrad, university provides these four things, the structure of success, its customers are willing to overlook outdated teaching practices. We acknowledge that even though it's not ideal, if we were left to our own devices we probably wouldn't persist long enough to learn anything significant, so we take the deal. It doesn't hurt that we get a bit of paper at the end of it.

My point is not about universities as such, but the power of providing the elements of implementation. The traditional undergraduate university degree is not best practice from an adult education point of view; far from it. But it does pretty well from an implementation perspective, by providing all the external elements of our primary implementation model.

The lesson we can learn from this is to make sure all these external elements are present in the projects we undertake. Throughout the rest of the book we will be unpacking all five elements across our personal lives, our teams and our organisations.

PART I

PERSONAL

Chapter 2

PERSONAL

——— OVERVIEW ———

I've missed more than 9000 shots in my career. I've lost almost 300 games. Twenty-six times, I've been trusted to take the game winning shot and missed. I've failed over and over and over again in my life. And that is why I succeed.

Michael Jordan, the greatest basketballer of all time

The new rules of management are about shifting from managing systems and processes for more efficiency, and managing people like they are part of the machine, to implementing projects that matter. And while we will come to how to do this in our teams and organisations, project creation and implementation start with you personally. How are you creating and implementing the projects that make up your life?

For Stone Age humans, just the process of surviving in a hostile and unpredictable environment was fully engaging. Any day you didn't get eaten was a good day, and being warm, dry and fed was a bonus. This struggle over hundreds of thousands, or perhaps millions, of years, predisposed us to engage in the type of action that would have ensured we survived in those circumstances. The hardware you are operating with is designed to help you survive as a hunter-gatherer a hundred thousand years ago. But if you're reading this book, your survival is pretty much a given. The fact that you are warm, dry and fed (not to mention that you haven't been eaten today) is nothing to write home about.

Being fulfilled today requires more than surviving: the game has changed to thriving, and the key to that is doing great work — implementing great projects.

It's why retirement sucks. Retirement should be great, shouldn't it? You have made your money; the kids have finally moved out; you don't have to go to work any more — you have looked after yourself so your body is still healthy and your mind is still active. Your only job now is to have fun. That should be a piece of cake. It should be great — but it sucks. Why? Because it turns out just having fun isn't fun. Doing great work is fun — that's what's fulfilling. Travelling, lawn bowls, golf, hobbies are all great things, but on their own they can feel empty.

Equally, fulfilment doesn't come from having more stuff. Australian houses grew 50 per cent bigger from 1985 to 2010, and yet there is no evidence that Australians are any happier with the extra rumpus room, two bathrooms and an extra bedroom.

A recent study also showed that the majority of Australians think that they will be happy on 20 per cent more income: people who earn 20 per cent less than you do believe they would be happy on your income. People on your income think they would be happy earning 20 per cent more. The people who earn that 20 per cent more, well they think they would be happy with just a further 20 per cent. Nothing is ever enough. While Spike Milligan famously said, 'I just want the chance to prove money doesn't buy happiness', study after study has proved that once your basic needs are met, more money doesn't result in more happiness and fulfilment.

So, if more free time, more stuff and more money don't provide fulfilment, what does? Science tells us that the answer is purpose, progress and autonomy. Of course these all come from implementing projects that matter. But, as we have seen, we're actually predisposed to take the type of actions that would have had us survive a few thousand centuries back. Unfortunately those aren't the same actions that will have us successfully implement our projects.

As we can see from the primary implementation model again (see figure 2.1), successfully implementing these projects requires changing our internal mindset, creating a powerful framework, enlisting the right support and setting up an appropriate accountability structure.

Figure 2.1: primary implementation model

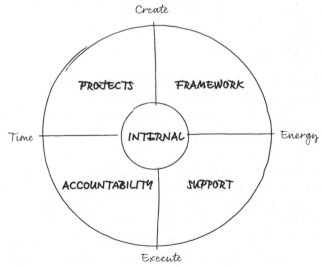

Internal

An implementation mindset is the internal component on the primary implementation model. It is integral to the creation and execution of projects that matter. While it's critical to get the external structures right, it's also important to look internally, and to foster the right mindset.

At the start of a project we need to embrace the risk of any meaningful undertaking. We need to be comfortable with the possibility of failing, and not let that possibility stop us from even starting. We need to choose our projects powerfully, and commit 100 per cent. Often we haven't really decided that we are in, and we don't give everything of ourselves. There is generally a phase in any major project when the going gets tough, and we need to persevere. This takes a certain internal fortitude, and this is often when our mindset is most challenged. Finally, we need to complete our projects—not just get 90 per cent done and move on.

Projects

Everything we do is an instinct, a response, a habit, a system or a project. The further along that spectrum, the more energy it takes and the bigger the payoff. Meaningful projects are where the magic lies.

At a personal level, successful people focus on making these projects a stretch, and getting out of their comfort zone. If we have developed an implementation mindset and are willing to fail, it means that we can launch ambitious projects that we may or may not be able to pull off. The projects that succeed are what ultimately make us successful, and the ones that fail will give us our greatest growth. All of them will lead to our fulfilment.

Framework

The framework we implement is made up of the context, the environment and the methodology that we operate within. It answers the questions of why, where and how we run our projects.

The framework for our personal implementation needs to be congruent with who we are and what we're about. If we are not clear about why we are embarking on a project, and if our motivation isn't aligned with our purpose and values, we will find that we sabotage ourselves.

Support

Don't try to do it all yourself—particularly if your projects are a stretch. You will need some support.

There are a number of support roles to fill around your significant projects: the mentors who can accelerate your journey; the friends who keep you true to who you are and what you do; the crew that you rely on to make stuff happen; and finally the promoters, who create positive noise around your projects.

Accountability

We are not wired for long-term projects because they require us to defer gratification. We are set up to take the actions that give us pleasure or avoid pain in the short term. Consequently an effective accountability structure can be very powerful in keeping us on track with the execution of our projects.

Accountability can be to ourselves, to our peers, to someone in a position of authority, or to the world at large. There are pros and cons at each level. It makes sense to determine the most effective level of accountability for each project.

Chapter 3

INTERNAL

——— MINDSET ———

A journey of a thousand miles starts with a single step.

Lao-tzu, the founder of philosophical Taoism

Every project goes through three distinct phases:

1 start

2 persevere

3 complete.

Typically, we have strengths and weaknesses at different phases, and it's valuable to reflect on which phase you are most comfortable, and where you need the most help. For instance, do you struggle with starting? My wife Trish calls herself a 'momentum chick': she says she's great when she gets going on something, but sometimes needs a bit of a shove to get started.

Or are you good at starting, but not so strong at persevering? As soon as you hit a roadblock, do you look for the next project to start? I have a friend who calls this 'the shiny object syndrome', because he is easily distracted by the next shiny object that comes along.

If you're good at starting and persevering, then maybe you're like me, and struggle with the last 5 per cent? When a project is basically done, and there's just the last bit of polishing or cleaning up to do before I can call it complete, I have already moved on emotionally. For me it takes discipline to do the last pieces and move the project from my active list to my complete list.

Knowing where you are weakest can give you an advantage, because you can develop strategies to get you through these sticking points and stay on track. Let's look at the three phases in a bit more detail.

Start

Getting going can be half the battle.

Choose your projects wisely; commit to them 100 per cent; and get going. Guy Kawasaki has written a whole book about this — *The Art of the Start* — which we will look at in a bit more detail in chapter 9.

Trish the 'momentum chick' has three different methods for tricking herself into getting started:

- *Do just 20 minutes.* She tells herself she only has to spend 20 minutes on the task or the project and then she can stop if she wants. She even sets an alarm for 20 minutes, and gives herself complete permission to stop after that, although for that 20 minutes she is not allowed any distractions. Inevitably by the time the alarm goes off she is engaged and she keeps going.

- *Start with the easiest things first.* This was one I used for this book. The thought of writing a book of 55 000 words can be a bit daunting. I started writing when we stopped in Bali for four days on the way through to Java, and my first milestone was 10 000 words by the time we left Bali. I pasted in 5000 words that I had written on the topic in other places. Even if they all needed editing, I suddenly felt I was underway. I had started.

- *Go to a coffee shop with your laptop.* This is a great way to lock yourself into getting started. Trish knows that if she sits down in a café and orders her favourite coffee (long black with hot milk on the side), suddenly getting started isn't so hard. And there isn't anything else to do, so it doesn't take as much energy.

Persevere

Do whatever it takes to do the work and keep going. There is a different energy required in the middle phase of a project. There is none of the excitement or the trepidation felt at the beginning of the project, when anything is possible, when we are deciding which mountain to climb. We have chosen the mountain, and the energy we need now is about persisting, about continuing to put one foot in front of the other.

You're 80 per cent there if you can recognise that you're not wired for this, and you put whatever you need in place to stick it out.

Derek Sivers is the founder of CD Baby, a business that he created by accident and sold a decade later for $22 million, and author of Amazon number-one bestseller *Anything You Want*. Here is what he says about perseverance:

> When I was 14 years old I had a guitar teacher who said you've got to learn how to sing, because if you don't, you're always going to be at the mercy of some asshole singer. I was the guitar player. He said—you've just got to learn to sing.

And I agreed. It kind of went with my introvert tendencies the fact that I didn't want to always have to be partnering with other people any time I wanted to make a song. So I was just determined I wanted to be a good singer.

And I started practising. I started taking voice lessons. I started just singing every opportunity I could get. I joined a band as lead singer. Everybody told me I was awful, but I didn't care because in my head it wasn't about that performance. It was about 'I'm on a multi-year journey to become a great singer.' So don't tell me hey, you're awful. You should go get a good singer. I wanted the criteria that would make me a better singer even if it took years.

So those are the choices I always took any time I was presented with a decision, I always chose the one that would make me a better singer. So I had a coffee house duo. I was a solo performer. I was the lead singer of a five-piece band. I even joined a circus and I was out there four days a week, singing kids songs to audiences of 500 kids. And I would sing on street corners and subways and I would sing without a sound system and get my voice to carry across a crowd just me and my guitar. And I still kept taking lessons, singing my arpeggios and long tones and scales and imitating Stevie Wonder and imitating Tom Waits — whatever it took.

And after 10 years of doing that people still told me, Derek, you're just not a singer. Just quit trying. You're obviously just not a singer. You need to find a real singer. But I didn't even let the comments get to me. I thought 'I know what I'm doing, I'm going to keep trying.' So yeah, it was about 15 years of persevering. I was about 29 years old the first time I was recording some stuff and listened back to my voice in the recording and I went yeah. That's actually really good. For the first time in my life after 15 years of trying I think I can say that that was a really good performance. I think I'm sounding okay now. So here it was 15 years later.

I think that being willing to make mistakes and being very comfortable with that is a huge competitive advantage. I think most people go through life kind of protecting the downside too much so that they don't get the advantage of the upside to things. Whereas if you're willing to just throw yourself out there and make a bunch of mistakes and not take any one of them personally, I think it has something to do with thinking of life in more of a long-term picture. If you see what you're doing as a multi-year long journey, then you don't let every little mistake bother you. They're just inconsequential.

Whereas if you're thinking short term and you think that today is all there is, or even this quarter is all there is, then of course you're going to be more risk averse, you're going to be too careful, you're not going to want to take chances because you just have to think short-term results. But if you're willing to think of things in the bigger picture, try all kinds of crazy stuff, and know that for every mistake you make that's an amazing lesson that you can use that you would never get if you didn't make that mistake.

I don't think of it as mistakes at all...Even if you started a project or a business or something and it went out of business, even that you couldn't call a failure until you see the results of what you learned in the process and what you are going to apply that to.

I just don't believe in failure. Once you know that, really you can just recklessly throw yourself into all kinds of things. Why not? Let's try this. Let's try that because every single thing you try is going to be another lesson that makes you smarter.

Here are my three keys to perseverance:

- *Box yourself in.* Psychologically, physically and emotionally create constraints for yourself. If you are going to spend three hours on a project, don't allow anything else in, or yourself out. Create a physical environment that allows you to focus—turn off your email, electronic tablet, phone, and so on—and just do the work. And don't ask yourself whether you feel like doing it or not: it is almost never a useful question to ask at this point in a project.

- *Give yourself permission to fail.* Keep choosing whether to fail the project or complete it. But it has to be one or the other—either fail it with no regrets, or give it 100 per cent.

- *Create milestones, victories and mini-projects along the way.* If you want to learn salsa, for instance, create milestones around the number of lessons you have attended, the number of hours you have put in, and the number of steps you have added to your repertoire. Make sure you celebrate these milestones along the way—little bits of progress is what keeps us going.

Complete

Don't stumble when you're 99 per cent of the way there. Get it finished, tick it off. Be clear about whether your project has been a success or failure. Celebrate and learn the lessons, and move the project to your completed list.

For the majority of our projects, most of the value comes when they are complete. A book that is 90 per cent done doesn't give me much reward compared with a published book out in the world. Yet for many of us this is the most confronting part—when our work goes out into the world, and we can be judged. It's the time when we have to confront whether the project was a success or a failure.

Finally, here are my three keys to completion:

- *Perfection is the enemy of completion.* Work out what is good enough, and get your project to that point, not to perfection. Get a first version complete and out in the world—you can always improve it later.

- *Create deadlines.* If I want to design a new workshop, I will set a date, sell it, and then when I know I have 20 people coming along in three weeks' time I will get to work on creating a great workshop.

- *Get comfortable with failure.* Recognise that if you are like most people, you're not comfortable with failure, *and* that it is stopping you getting things finished. We have been trained over a long time that it's not okay to fail, so we need some reprogramming. The rest of this chapter has a number of useful strategies and beliefs for getting more comfortable with failure.

As you can see in figure 3.1 (overleaf), there are six elements to creating an implementation mindset:

1 Fail 50 per cent

2 Commit completely

3 Value shakti

4 Fight for three

5 Do what you say

6 Publish ruthlessly.

Figure 3.1: implementation mindset model

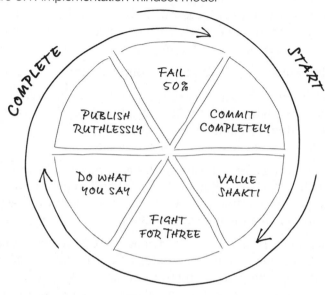

Where your strengths and weaknesses lie in the different phases of a project will dictate which of these elements you should concentrate on. For example, if you are weak at starting projects, focus on Fail 50 per cent, Commit completely and Value shakti. If you are weak at the persevere phase, focus on Value shakti, Fight for three and Do what you say. And if you are weak at completing, focus on Do what you say, Publish ruthlessly and Fail 50 per cent.

Fail 50 per cent

A successful life, career, relationship, year, quarter or anything else is a result of how many projects you have successfully implemented. This is a really important point. When you look back at your year, you will judge it by the projects you implemented. (I will come back to this in chapter 4).

In baseball, a batting percentage is the number of hits you get as a percentage of 'at bats'. A good major league batter will bat 250—that means that out of 1000 'at bats', he will get a hit 250 times. So 25 per cent of the time a player walks up to the plate, they will end up hitting the ball and at least getting to first base. A great batter will bat 300. In baseball this is the main measure of your value as a batter—the percentage of times you are successful.

In baseball there are a limited number of 'at bats'. A typical major league batter will have around 600 at bats per season, and so the number of hits they get is a direct result of their batting percentage. But this is not a good metaphor for life. In life, the number of projects you launch is not limited. So success is more a result of the number and quality of projects that you launch rather than the percentage of those that are successful.

For example, if over a year I launch five major projects and I am 100 per cent successful, I will have implemented five successful projects. If over the same year you launch 50 projects, and have a 50 per cent success rate, you will have successfully implemented 25 projects, and had a much more successful year than me.

Unfortunately, school is more like baseball than life. In school there are a set number of assessments, tests and projects. We are trained not to fail these. Failing 50 per cent of your subjects or your exams is not a good strategy for school. So we learn to try not to fail anything.

However for life, failing 50 per cent of your projects is a great strategy. Aiming to fail 50 per cent of your projects is the perfect way to embrace the risk inherent in any worthwhile project. It also helps you launch better projects. If you are considering an edgy project and your mindset is about not failing, you will probably let it pass you by. However, if you are aiming to fail 50 per cent of your projects you are not attached to succeeding with each one. You have the freedom to start projects that are at the perimeter of what you think is possible—projects that light you up, challenge you, and that aren't safe.

This mindset also helps you *complete* projects. If you are not scared of failing, it's much easier to go hard for the finish line, without being worried about what it will mean if you complete a project and fail. The strategy then becomes to make our failures as cheap, quick, small and as private as possible, and to protect your self-talk at the same time (more on this in the next section).

Aim to fail 50 per cent of your major projects or goals. Each month or quarter, when reviewing your progress, make that your benchmark.

I love to ski, although truth be told I'm not that good at it. But I'll have a crack at skiing down just about anything. If, at the end of a full day's skiing, I realise I haven't fallen over all day, I think to myself that I probably wasn't trying hard enough, or pushing myself enough. I was playing too safe. It's the same if I get to the end of a month or a quarter and I have achieved all my goals. It probably means that I set the bar too low and didn't have enough edgy goals and projects on the go that were going to test me and light up my world.

Commit completely

The only way to be in the persevere stage of any project is to be 100 per cent committed.

Before the birth of our first daughter, Trish and I went to our first antenatal class. Trish was 29 weeks pregnant at the time, and there were about 20 other couples at similar stages in the class. It was a group unlike any other I have been a part of: 20 obviously pregnant women, and 20 even more obviously nervous blokes. We watched a bunch of videos of different women in different stages of labour and then one of an actual birth. I have to say, it looked a bit different from how it's portrayed in the movies! I could feel the anxiety levels in the room rising as we went through the class, and at one point I asked jokingly 'It's too late to change our minds, isn't it?' Of course everyone laughed—I think there were a few others in the room thinking the same thing. But at that point we were all 100 per cent committed. There was no turning back.

Everybody has self-worth issues. We have all had experiences that had their impact on us when we were growing up, and we all have a little voice in the back of our head that tells us every now and then that we're not good enough. Different people deal with this in different ways: some become over-confident to compensate; others do the reverse. But it's there to some degree in all of us.

Often we don't commit to serious goals and projects because of the risk of failing. 'What will it mean about me if I really go for it and don't get there? What will other people think? What will I think?'

Here are a few useful ideas for dealing with a fear of failure:

- *No one else cares.* Really. Everyone else is so caught up in their own life and their own stuff that *your* victories and failures are of only passing interest.

- *No regrets.* Lots of studies report that what people regret most in life is not what they failed at, but what they didn't attempt. When you're sitting on a rocking chair on your deck in your old age (it seems to be only in the movies that the elderly pass their time rocking away on decks, but you get the picture), looking back on your life, would you rather remember that you gave this a red-hot go and came up short, or that you didn't make it to the starting line?

- *Failure is a part of life.* All really successful people have a healthy and intimate relationship with failure, and most have failed hard and often. There are dozens of quotes I could have put here about failing and persevering—about Edison's 1000 light globes that didn't work, about the numerous setbacks and failures US President Abraham Lincoln experienced before his eventual election, and so on. Getting comfortable with failure is a critical part of success. Any worthwhile aspiration bears with it the possibility of failing, but the real failure is when you let that possibility take you out of the game. Factor in a 50 per cent failure rate. Expect to hit 50 per cent of your big goals and launch enough projects that matter for winning half of them to be enough to have you thrilled.

The thing to do at the start of a project is to commit 100 per cent. Make sure that you are clear about what the project is—what you are aiming to achieve by when: what framework you are operating in—what's the context, methodology and environment; and choose powerfully either to do it or not to do it. But be clear with yourself that if you choose this project, you will be 100 per cent committed, and give it everything you've got. Treat the project like a pregnancy—once you're committed, there's no turning back.

This can seem to contradict my earlier point about failing 50 per cent, and making our failures as cheap, quick, small and private as possible. Pete, how can you tell me to treat the project like a pregnancy and to commit 100 per cent, but then be willing to fail half of them? It is a paradox.

Up until the point we decide to fail a project, and pull the pin, we have to be 100 per cent committed. Treating it like it's life and death.

When we watch a movie, we create the illusion in our mind that it's real, the characters are alive, and the plot is really happening. Then at the end we remember that it was only a movie. It's the same with our projects. While we are in them, we create the illusion that it's life or death—that this project matters way more than it actually does. Our mindset and way of being is 100 per cent committed. Then, at certain points, we step back and remind ourselves that it's just a project that we made up; then we review the progress and decide whether to fail it or not. If we decide to continue, we go back to our illusion, and commit 100 per cent again. If we choose to fail a project, we do it powerfully and learn the lessons, but don't beat ourselves up about it. Remember, our job is to fail half our projects. We then get back up, and create the next project—move on to the next game.

Value shakti

Shakti is a Sanskrit word that means more than energy—it's something like your life force, your spirit, your energy and your essence all rolled into one. It's a beautiful concept that my friend Robert Rabbin introduced me to.

Implementation takes shakti. Big projects take all of you—you can't just show up and go through the motions. Ten minutes that you bring all of yourself to, when your shakti is high, and your energy is strong, can achieve bigger results than a day or a week of just putting in time, and going through the motions.

Valuing shakti means recognising this, and being able to assess your energy levels and act accordingly.

Implementation is about creating and executing projects that matter. The creation part takes a different level of energy (for me, anyway), while there are some parts of the execution that can generally be done with lower energy levels. I will design projects and do the hard thinking in the morning when my energy is better. In the evenings, if I'm working, it will be on things that I find easier.

Valuing shakti also means doing things that give you energy, and not doing things that don't. How you eat, exercise and sleep, your environment and whom you spend time with, all impact your energy. It's worth becoming conscious of this, and doing more of the things that raise your shakti, and less of the things that don't.

One of the biggest inputs to your shakti is the conversations that take place inside your head. The quality of your self-talk, the little voice inside your head that gives you a running commentary on how you are going, is critical to your ability to implement successfully.

I believe that how confident I am about achieving something is not an objectively accurate measure, but is often a self-fulfilling prophecy. When I was 27 I started a business coaching practice. While I had worked for a few years as a business consultant with Accenture, I had never run a business, and I had never been a coach. If I knew then what I know now, I would never have started, but at the time I figured I would be pretty good at it, and I would be able to work out what I didn't know.

Objectively, my confidence was misplaced. I had no idea how I was going to get clients, how to price my offering or how to structure a coaching program. I also didn't realise the impact that having no experience in business or as a coach would have on my credibility. But in this case, ignorance was bliss.

Subjectively my confidence wasn't misplaced. It allowed me to persist long enough to be successful. And after persevering through a very tough first year, things started to turn around. From year two on I had a coaching practice that was generating a six-figure income.

Most of the time you are your own worst critic, because you are not a good judge of your own success or your ability. Find a more objective measure of your ability to implement, and calibrate your self-talk accordingly. A key to this is to accurately assess why a project failed. Left to its own devices, your inner critic will find some fatal flaw in your character that led to the failure.

Use the primary implementation model (see figure 2.1, p. 23) in this book to find another reason. Typically, one of these characteristics applies: the project wasn't structured properly as a project; you didn't have the right framework for executing it; you didn't have adequate support in place; or you didn't create an appropriate accountability structure. Sometimes it wasn't the right project—you didn't really choose it and weren't fully committed to it. Or it might have been one of the 50 per cent of projects that was meant to fail.

Fight to make your self-talk empowering rather than limiting. I believe that you can achieve way more than you think you can. Your potential is almost limitless. Calibrate your self-talk to that, and then fight to keep it there.

My dad shared a great story with me that he read in *Putting Out of Your Mind* by performance consultant Bob Rotella. It's about Jack Nicklaus, the greatest golfer to ever play the game, and the quality of his self-talk:

As part of a talk he was giving, Nicklaus had said, 'I have never three-putted, or missed from inside five feet, on the final hole of a tournament.' Professional golfers usually only need two putts, and normally only one from within five feet. Occasionally they slip up, but the final hole of a 72-hole tournament is the ultimate test of their nerve.

At question time a member of the audience challenged Nicklaus, saying that he had watched a recent tournament and that Nicklaus had missed a three-foot putt on the last hole.

Nicklaus replied that the man was wrong and restated his assertion. The man offered to send him a video tape, but Nicklaus said that this was unnecessary as he was there himself, and restated for the third time that he had never three-putted, or missed from inside five feet on the final green of a tournament.

After the talk the audience member came up to Dr Rotella and asked why Jack Nicklaus couldn't just admit that he was wrong.

Rotella asked the man if he played golf, what his handicap was, and whether, if he missed a short putt on the last hole of a tournament, he would remember it and admit it. It turned out that the man was an average weekend golfer with a 16 handicap, and yes, he would remember and admit it if he missed a short putt on the last hole of a tournament.

Rotella then said to the man: 'So let me get this straight, you're a 16 handicapper, and Jack Nicklaus is the greatest golfer ever, and you want Jack to think like you?' The man had no answer.

I love this story. Jack Nicklaus's test for what to believe is not what's true, but what's useful. There is a whole philosophical debate we could get into about the nature of truth, but the point is we have a lot of beliefs—particularly about ourselves—that are very much in the category of 'not useful'.

Likewise we want the conversations that happen outside our head—the ones with other people involved—to provide inspiration and energy, particularly when a project is in its early stages and is just finding its legs. For this reason I am very selective about the people I talk to about new projects. When a project is very new, and the possibility is still fragile, I will avoid telling people who I think might crush the possibility, or damage my mindset and self-talk, and reduce my shakti.

Fight for three

You can't put in 80 hours a week of significant, creative, real work. We make the mistake of putting in the time and thinking that that means we are productive.

When I run workshops, I know that adults can absorb information in one form and learn effectively for about 10 minutes before the capacity to take in new information starts to drop off. So if I have been talking for 10 minutes, I will change something. I will ask a question, get participants to discuss what I have talked about, go to an exercise, or something else. I also won't conduct a workshop for more than 90 minutes without a break.

If I am training other people, I am very conscious and scientific about determining the most effective way for participants to work and learn. Yet when I am on my own, I can be much less rigorous and methodical about the structure that I work in.

I know that if I have a one-hour window, and five things that I need to do, I'm like a machine. I will be focused, efficient, productive and effective. But give me a whole afternoon to do the same five things, and I will start by checking my emails; I might check out the news online; see if there is anything on Facebook … and suddenly it's been half an hour, and I haven't really done anything, and the whole afternoon can go on like that.

Fight for three sessions a day of productive work on your big projects. Three 30-minute to one-hour blocks of your best work is a great day's work, and much better than 16 hours of responding to requests, shuffling emails, following systems and getting stuff done. When I have discretionary time (that is, I'm not delivering a program), I aim for three productive sessions of work, and three positive outcomes. Sometimes I have to fight for it, because honestly I don't feel like it. I would rather respond to stuff than do real, hard work.

Meetings don't count. Meetings generally don't require the same effort to get started. Once the meeting is scheduled I know I will show up, and we're all good. It doesn't take the same effort as sitting down to write for an hour.

If possible I aim to get all three sessions done in the morning, and ideally before 10 am. If by 10 am I have already done a good day's work, it puts me in a great space for the rest of the day. Typically I will schedule meetings and calls in the afternoon so that I can do my own work in the morning.

After you have put in your three sessions, go back to your task list or knock off and go to the movies.

I also use the idea of fighting for three on a larger scale. Each quarter I pick three projects in my personal life and three in my business life that I am going to focus on. Three that I am going to fight for. In my project portfolio (a concept discussed in the next chapter) there are many more projects than this, but these are the ones that rise above the rest for 90 days.

Do what you say

This is all about personal integrity, and it is something that all truly productive people, all great implementers, have a level of mastery in. My good friend and mentor Robert Rabbin, who is also the best-selling author of eight books and a brilliant speaker, wrote recently on his blog:

> After some 35 years of working in my teacher's organization and then working with numerous diverse organizations and professionals, I discovered a single principle the practice of which definitely increases self-awareness, while at the same time creating an organizational culture that fosters interpersonal connection, trust, reliability, accountability, enthusiasm, wholeheartedness and all kinds of other good things. One principle does all this. And I want to share that with you now.
>
> Do what you say you will do.

I *love* it!

I believe that the single biggest thing you can do to be more productive, successful and fulfilled is to keep your promises.

It is absolutely critical through the persevere and completion phases of a project — and just about everywhere else in life — to do what you say.

We all know people who say they will do something, be somewhere or look after something, and inside we think, 'We'll see'. And there are other people who, when they say they will do something, we know it's going to happen — we could take that commitment to the bank. Much more powerful to be in the second group.

I have recently engaged a new financial planner — Matt. He had come highly recommended, and he knew his stuff. But here's what sold me. The morning of our meeting he had woken up at 3.30 am to go to the gym. Sounds a bit insane, but he had made a commitment to go to the gym 100 days in a row. And this particular day he was playing golf at 6 am before work, had a function after work, and the only way he could make it was get up at some stupid hour of the morning.

Again, I *love* it. Here's a guy who keeps his word, even when it's completely unreasonable to do so, and even though his promise was only to himself. It's easy to keep your word when it only takes reasonable actions to do so. The test comes when it requires setting the alarm at 3.30 am to do so.

Two things happen when you make a commitment to keep your word, and to do what you say. The first is that you become much more conscious of what comes out your mouth. You start to pay much more attention to what you say. The second is that you then become much more careful about what you promise, and make sure you only make the promises you intend to keep.

Michael Port, best-selling author of *Book Yourself Solid*, talks about a bonus that comes from integrity. He says that the best way to build your confidence is to make commitments and fulfil them—to do what you say. I agree. So not only is doing what you say critical to creating an implementation mindset and fulfilling on your important projects, you will also feel better about yourself!

Publish ruthlessly

Seth Godin, creator of permission marketing, describes this concept as shipping. In his book *Poke the Box*—a call to action for personal and work initiatives—Godin concentrates on the importance of moving forward and putting your work to the test in public. He calls this commitment to implementation 'shipping', and explains that the risk of doing nothing is far greater than the risk that your effort might fail:

> It's extremely difficult to find smart people willing to start useful projects. Because sometimes what you start doesn't work. The fact that it doesn't work every time should give you confidence, because it means you're doing something that frightens others.

So, finish version 1.0 of your project and get it out into the world. Declare your intent at the start, even if it's just to yourself or a few of your supporters, and publish your result at the end. Be ruthless with yourself about getting projects done and the results out.

Writing a blog is a great way to build this muscle. If you are going to blog every week about a subject that you are an expert or interested in, you are forced to publish weekly. Even if you're not inspired, or don't have the time, publish something anyway. If you do this for one year, not only will you have practised publishing ruthlessly, you will also have built a body of work in your area.

Of course publishing isn't just about writing: it's a metaphor for the completion of any project. It is powerful to have some ceremony at the end, something to 'publish'. I had a project to get a black belt in aikido, and my black belt grading was 'publishing' in this case. I invited a bunch of family and close friends to watch, and we went out to a great Japanese restaurant afterwards to celebrate. If I wanted to learn salsa, I would have some sort of performance as the event to 'publish' the project. Likewise, if my project were to renovate my house, I'd have a dinner party or house warming party to mark the completion of the project.

In many domains of life, finished and out in the world is better than perfect. The first version of this book is a good example of this. I had a hard deadline (a keynote speech I was delivering) and even though the book was only 80 per cent of where I wanted it to be, I published (that version was self published). I only printed 200 copies and fortunately, one of those copies ended up in the hands of Lucy Raymond, Acquisitions Editor at Wiley. While it wasn't perfect, it was good enough for Wiley to want to publish it. That meant I then had the opportunity to do the final 20 per cent I wanted to do and it went into the book you are holding in your hands now.

I love the idea of version 1.0. Whenever I have a new website or a new offering, I set a deadline for version 1.0. The first working version. A version that is good enough, like the first version of this book. It gives me something to do with the part of my brain that wants everything to be perfect. I can have an idea, and say great, that can go in version 2.0. Right now I need to get version 1.0 up and out in the world.

IN SUMMARY

An implementation mindset is critical for making projects happen. We all have different strengths and weaknesses across the three phases of a project: start, persevere and complete. And there are different things we can do to improve our performance across the three phases.

Three things to do

1 Identify which of the three phases—start, persevere or complete—is your weakest.

2 Look at the implementation mindset model (see figure 3.1, p. 34) and identify the three elements of that phase.

3 Take the three corresponding actions:

- *Fail 50 per cent*. This is a big idea: reprogramming your mind that your job is now to fail half your projects. Talk to three people in your life about this idea.

- *Commit completely*. List the active projects in your life, and check if you have committed completely to them. If you haven't, pull them off your list.

- *Value shakti*. Schedule something once a week that is purely about lifting your shakti.

- *Fight for three*. Identify the three professional projects and three personal projects that you are fighting for over the next 90 days.

- *Do what you say*. For 30 days focus on keeping every promise you make. When you can't keep a promise, let the person know before it's due.

- *Publish ruthlessly*. Identify three projects in your world that are 90 per cent complete and in the next 30 days be ruthless about getting them finished.

Chapter 4

PROJECTS

When I have finished, if the solution is not beautiful,
I know it is wrong.

Buckminster Fuller, inventor and visionary

We can only ever do one of five things. Everything we do is an instinct, a response, a habit, a system or a project (and projects are what rock). This is a big idea. If you look at the model in figure 4.1 (overleaf), you will see a line through the middle of habit. To the left of the line is what all animals do (including us). It's only humans, however, that occupy the ground to the right of the line.

It's an interesting exercise to look at how much of your life is spent in each. How much time is purely instinctual (spent, for instance, sleeping)? How much time do you spend responding to external stimuli? Do you show up to work and respond to requests, emails, phone calls and meetings all day long? How much of your day is habitual and happens on autopilot? How much of your time is spent following systems and procedures? And finally, how much time is spent on your projects?

Let's look at each of these in a bit more detail.

Figure 4.1: personal projects model

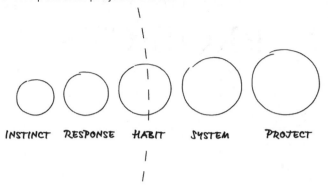

Instinct

We are born with our instincts, and everything else comes later. We have evolved to have instincts before anything else. A newborn baby placed on her mother's stomach will instinctively wriggle up and start suckling.

Things that you do that are instinctual don't require any thought. They just happen. Breathing is an instinct. The fight-or-flight response is an instinct. Given these are the things that happen without any thought, they don't get too much attention in this book.

Response

The phone rings and we pick it up. The traffic light turns red so we put our foot on the brake pedal. The alarm goes off and we get out of bed (or groan and dive under the pillow). These are all responses to some kind of external stimulus. We respond at three levels: feeling, thinking and acting. If you say something to me I might have an emotional response. I would then think about it and probably say something back.

We, like all animals, are wired to respond to external stimuli. It doesn't take much energy or effort to respond. The action itself may take energy and effort, but the act of responding comes very easily.

Habit

Over time we develop habits, both consciously and unconsciously. Brushing your teeth might be a habit; driving to work is a habit. Habits are great because they reduce the amount of energy required to get things done. Imagine if brushing your teeth wasn't a habit. Every day you had to work out what was the best way to clean your teeth, which implements to use, how long to do it for, and then do it. It would be exhausting.

Some of our habits serve us, and some don't. It is worth identifying which habits we want to develop, which we want to keep, and which we want to get rid of. It's been said that it takes 30 days to replace an old habit with a new one.

I used to have the habit of putting one teaspoon of sugar in my tea and coffee. Angela, my dentist, told me it was not a good idea for my teeth, and asked me to try not having sugar for 30 days. For the first week my tea and coffee tasted really bitter, but after that it became normal, and now if I taste coffee with sugar, it's too sweet. I developed a new habit.

Systems

Josh Kaufman, author of *The Personal MBA: Master the Art of Business*, defines systems this way:

> A system is a process made explicit and repeatable—a series of steps that has been formalised in some way. Systems can be written or diagrammed, but they are always externalised in some way. The primary benefit of creating a system is that you

can examine the process and make improvements. By making each step in the process explicit, you can understand how the core processes work, how they're structured, how they affect other processes and systems, and how you can improve the system over time.

Systems are a bit like conscious habits. A documented procedure is a way of reducing the energy it takes to get something done. I am way into systems. For example, I have a documented system for what I need to do before delivering a keynote address. Rather than creating a project out of it, I just refer to the procedure. The system tells me that I need to check through the slides, make sure they all work, and then create a backup in both PowerPoint and Keynote software on a data stick, which I wear on a lanyard around my neck.

I travel a fair bit, so I also have systems for what to pack. It's a different list for an interstate work trip than for a ski trip or a trip to Bali. But having all of these documented reduces the amount of energy and stress it takes me to pack. It has the bonus of meaning I will never get to a hotel room and realise that I forgot to pack my phone charger. Unfortunately I have yet to work out a system to make sure I don't leave my phone charger in the hotel room. I have a bad habit of grabbing my phone off the charger in the morning, packing and leaving the charger behind!

Systems reduce redundant thinking, inefficient time and wasted energy—and create space for projects.

Projects

Your success, your meaning and your legacy all come down to creating and fulfilling awesome projects. If, at the end of your life, you look back and reflect on your success, it will come down to the important projects you implemented. If you want to get a greater sense of fulfilment in your life, take on more projects that matter to you. This is what thriving in the information age is all about. Great projects are the key to everything.

So what is a project? In *Getting Things Done*, time management guru David Allen defines a project as 'any commitment that takes more than one step to complete'. Organising the family holiday or inviting a group of friends over for a dinner party are both projects. Heading out to buy the groceries can be a project. These aren't the sorts of projects I'm talking about, however.

Important projects are the ones that take effort and commitment, and that can change the course of your life. Some of the important projects that I have completed, in no particular order, have been:

- having a family
- running my own business
- writing a best-selling book
- doing well enough in high school to be able to choose any university I wanted to attend
- cycling around Victoria and South Australia with a bunch of friends
- organising a bike ride to raise $50 000 for charity
- getting married
- backpacking around Europe for six months
- completing my university degrees
- running the Apollo Bay Half Marathon.

Some important projects that are still in progress for me are:

- getting my third dan in aikido by the age of 40

- helping 1000 Australian bookkeepers through Pure Bookkeeping—a business I have a 50 per cent stake in
- buying one property a year for 10 years
- achieving financial independence before the age of 42
- raising a healthy, happy daughter who knows she is completely loved
- speaking Spanish fluently.

Fulfilment in life comes from the implementation of important project that mean something to us. There is a magic to projects—to setting a challenging 'what by when'.

What all this means

As we move to the right along the personal projects model shown in figure 4.1 (p. 50), things get harder. Instincts take no effort at all. Habits are only marginally more difficult. All the way along to the right, where projects lie, we reach the most difficult activities. Projects take the most effort, the most energy and the most shakti, and are the most confronting. Projects have the greatest potential for failure, and bring all the emotional and psychological fallout that comes with that.

The reason that projects are so difficult is that we are not wired for projects. As I have said earlier, we were designed to survive as hunter-gatherers, not to thrive in the modern world. If we were designed to thrive on psychological stress, projects would be easy, while reacting when a tiger crossed our path not so easy. Unfortunately, it's the other way around.

But it's worth doing whatever it takes to build your project muscle, and your competency at executing projects.

You are your projects. When you reflect on your year, on your month, on your career, on your relationships, and on the various roles in your life, you will assess the projects, not the instincts or habits. What were the important things that you did? What did you accomplish? What challenges did you overcome? What are you proud of? What were your important projects?

In a way it's fitting that projects aren't too easy. Life is better when there is an appropriate level of challenge. It's why I plan to never retire. While I have a project to be financially independent that is nearing completion, I don't plan on taking up lawn bowls and never working again. I know I would go crazy without the challenge—without some great projects in my life.

You have a finite amount of energy, of shakti, at your disposal. You want to maximise that amount, but it does have a limit. Consequently you need to get everything done with as little energy as possible. The secret to this is moving everything you do as far to the left as possible.

If I didn't have a system that I used to pack, every time I went away packing would be a mini-project. I would have to work out what I needed, think about what I was going to do and remember what I used last time. This is what my wife Trish does. And while she travels a little less than I do, packing is always stressful for her. For me it's easy; I just follow my system.

For part of the time I was writing this book Trish and I were living in Indonesia, learning Indonesian. It would have been possible for us to learn Indonesian ourselves without coming to a language class. There are websites, programs, CDs, and so on—I have no doubt it can be done. But it would be a significant project. By going to Indonesia, and enrolling in classes, we took a major project and turned it into a series of responses. We just had to show up to class and respond to the stimulus our teachers gave us. We were then told what homework to do.

It's the same with exercising while we were there. We were there for a month, away from our normal structures and routines. It's also very hot there and the streets aren't conducive to running. It would have been very easy for our fitness to go out the window for a month. So Trish found a gym in a hotel around the corner from where we were staying and we joined for the month. We committed to each other that we would go every day before breakfast, and so created external accountability to each other.

The first time I walked into the gym I felt a wave of resistance. What was I going to do? There were all these weights and strength machines in one room, a bunch of cardio machines in another, an aerobics room and a pool. I was overwhelmed and didn't know where to start. I didn't have a system, or anything to respond to. I walked into the weights room, and there were about 20 different machines (most of which I didn't know how to use), a television blaring in Indonesian, and a whole lot of people who looked like they knew exactly how to use the machines. I walked out of the weights room and went and sat on an exercise bike. At least I knew how to use that.

But the next day I still didn't know where to start. I actually wanted to do strength training. So I braved the weights room again and decided I would create a system. One day for arms and shoulders. One day for back, chest and abs, and one day for legs. I picked five exercises for each day, and did three sets of each. I had my system.

From then on it was relatively easy, and some of the machines that I didn't know how to use turned out to be really cool. They have this sit-up machine that replicates a sit up, but you can increase the weight. Normally my training is a bit more primal—body weight, push-ups, chin-ups, squats and so on. I was actually starting to have fun training a bit differently and using all the machines.

There were two key components in making exercising happen, and then to making it relatively easy. The first was the external accountability. Because Trish and I had agreed and committed to each other that we would go every day, we did. If it had just been my commitment to myself it would have been much easier to have a conversation with myself about all the reasons why it wasn't a good idea, or why this particular morning, blah, blah, blah. I'm sure you know the conversations in your head that I'm talking about. Because Trish was coming too I couldn't very well say, 'Trish, I'm a bit overwhelmed about where to start, so let's give it a miss.' That was central to getting to the gym (I will talk more about accountability in chapter 7).

Then the key to making exercising relatively easy was moving each session from a project to a system. Once I had set up my system, when I arrived I didn't have to think about what to do, I just had to follow my system.

To make it easier again I could have engaged a personal trainer. That would have brought it one rung further down the scale to responding. It takes less energy to just do what the trainer tells me than it does to do it myself.

If you follow a system or respond to the same set of stimuli enough times something will become a habit. Running (at least in Australia) is now a habit for me. When I'm on the road I pack my running gear (it's part of my packing system) and I will go for a run almost on autopilot. It's a habit that doesn't take much energy now. Well, the run itself takes energy, but getting started doesn't.

Projects that stretch us

If there is one key word that I think of when I think about projects in the personal domain it's the word 'stretch'. What do I mean by that? Well, each of us is capable of much more than we think. So if we get into the habit of launching more projects than we think we can complete, and launch projects that stretch us, we will end up with some remarkable projects, and more projects completed for the year than if we simply played it safe.

In aikido we spend a lot of time in *seiza*. That's how we sit when we are waiting for a technique to be demonstrated, and we also actually practise techniques from a kneeling position. Back in the day in Japan, you needed to be able to handle someone coming at you with a knife when you were innocently sitting, hanging out (in seiza), minding your own business.

Unfortunately I'm not designed for kneeling. I'm all good standing, and I'm a machine when it comes to sitting—give me a chair or a couch, and I can go all day. But kneeling, not so much. So after 30 seconds or so when my knees started to hurt a bit and I started to get a bit uncomfortable, I switched to sitting cross-legged. After a couple of years of that I decided to try an experiment. Rather than pulling out as soon as I started to get uncomfortable, I would wait until the pain got to seven or eight out of 10. Then a strange thing happened. It took longer and longer for the pain to get to that level, until it got to the point where it almost never did—I could sit in seiza for as long as I needed.

It's the same with getting better at anything. To get comfortable with selling, I had to have conversations that weren't comfortable to start with. To get comfortable speaking in front of groups, I had to be uncomfortable to start with. If you want to get stronger you won't do it lifting weights that are comfortable. You have to be willing to be a bit uncomfortable.

The idea of being willing to tolerate a discomfort level of seven or eight out of 10 is not a bad way to think about it. To grow or improve in any domain of your life or your business, you have to be willing to be a bit uncomfortable.

It's the same with our projects—we want projects that stretch us and take us out of our comfort zone; projects that have a chance of failing and are at the edge of what we think we can achieve.

I invite you to view your life as a series of projects, and to see yourself as the manager of a portfolio of projects in the different domains of your life (this is an idea of Lauren Keller Johnson, who talks about a project portfolio in an organisational context, and whose work we will come across in chapter 14). It's a way to design your life the way you want to live it.

Your life is a portfolio of projects, and you are managing that portfolio. It's a big idea. Most of us spend most of our time responding to external things, running our habits and following systems—not creating and executing the projects that matter.

If your primary job in leading your life is designing and managing a portfolio of projects, what would you do differently?

I have a mind map on my computer of all the projects in my life, organised into different domains—it means I can see my whole portfolio on one page. At the highest level the mind map is how I organise my life. There are projects that are active now, and projects that are for 'some day'. There are the three personal and the three professional projects that I'm 'fighting for' this quarter. I can click on any project and see the purpose, the specific outcome and the date.

At the end of every quarter I review my 'someday' projects, and decide if it's time to make any of them active. I also pick the projects that I'm going to focus on—to fight for—over the next 90 days.

IN SUMMARY

The quality of your life is a reflection of the quality of the projects you are implementing. Think about the domains of your life—such as health, relationships, family, career, business and finance. If there is a domain that you are not achieving success in and not feeling happy and fulfilled in, review the projects you have in that domain. And implement some better ones!

Three things to do

1 Track how much of your time is spent in instinct, response, habit, systems and projects.

2 Create a portfolio of all the projects in your life (you can download a template from www.newrulesofmanagement.com).

3 Pick three of your projects that you are fighting for, and fill out the Projects on a Page template from the book's website (you can download it from www.newrulesofmanagement.com).

Chapter 5

— FRAMEWORK —

The best way to predict the future is to invent it.

Alan Kay, pioneering computer scientist

All of our projects, and everything that we implement, sits within an overall framework. The framework answers the questions of why we implement, how we do it, and where. The framework is made up of our context, our environment and our method.

Within the personal domain, the focus for our framework is congruence — we need to make sure that the context, the environment and the methodology are aligned to what we really want to achieve. Wants often sit at the subconscious level and may not be spoken out loud or admitted to consciously. However, our subconscious is much more powerful than our conscious mind. If we are not aligned with a project at a deeper level, and we haven't really authentically chosen it, chances are it will fail.

If we remember back to our primary implementation model (see figure 2.1, p. 23), framework lives in the top right quarter.

The implementation framework model (see figure 5.1) shows us the critical elements in creating a powerful framework.

Figure 5.1: implementation framework model

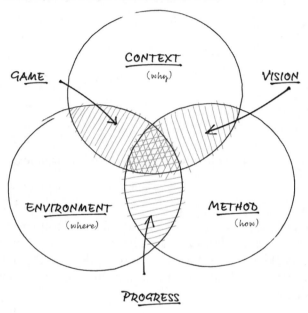

Context: why

Our context is, at the highest level, why we are doing the project. If I am launching a project to get fit, I might have a number of possible motivations. Perhaps I want to lose weight. Maybe I want to look better, or I might want to feel fitter and healthier. Maybe I have had a health scare, and it's about not being sick; or maybe at a higher level it's about family — I want to have more energy for my family.

For me running is about serving my clients. Whether I am leading a workshop or delivering a keynote address, I want to give 100 per cent. The people who have paid to come and spend time learning from me deserve my absolute best. So, I need to be fit enough to maintain my energy all day. That's why I run. It's strange, but that's a stronger motivation for me, and a more powerful context, than my own health and fitness.

It's very useful to externalise this context. When we see it on paper in front of us, we can ask the question 'Is this congruent with who I am? With my goals and my purpose? Have I really chosen this project?'

The weaker the context, the more likely we are to fail. If I'm running because someone told me I need to exercise more, and that's my context, running is unlikely to last long. Likewise, if I am running to lose weight, but I'm ambivalent about that goal, the project will probably fail.

As I said earlier, the unconscious part of our brain is much more powerful than our conscious mind, and most of what we do occurs at the subconscious level. All our skills, habits, values and beliefs are owned and driven by our unconscious mind, with perhaps only 10 per cent of what we do in a day being consciously driven. Things we do often, beliefs we have had since childhood, and behaviours we learned as kids have more pull on us than recently acquired activities, beliefs or behaviours, and that's because they have become unconscious through repetition.

Things we associate with unconscious behaviours act as triggers. These triggers can either work for us or against us. Managing our environmental and behavioural triggers can have a really positive impact on productivity. Sometimes, even making small changes in the environment can have a large impact on our biochemistry and our unconscious responses.

Environment: where

To create an environment that helps us implement our projects, we need to focus on making a space that is highly productive. A productive environment takes into account the tools, space, colour, stimulus and electronic environments required to complete a project.

Our environment is a much more powerful factor in our capacity to implement than we realise. Science has shown that exposure to the natural environment, even just a picture of it, makes us feel more relaxed, which increases creativity.

Janetta McCoy from Arizona State University and Gary Evans from Cornell conducted a great experiment to demonstrate this (which they published in *Handbook of Work Stress*, 1998). They set a creativity task (putting together a collage) for a control group do in a sterile room. They then altered the environment by putting pictures of nature up in the room and repeated the task with second group. The group that had pictures of nature in the room performed more creatively on the test.

I love this experiment because none of us would expect it. Imagine I asked you to perform a creative task, and put you in a room with no windows. Then the next day I put you in the same room, and asked you to perform another creative task, but this time I had put up a poster of a waterfall on the wall, and put a pot plant in the corner. The second time around chances are you would perform significantly better (when they performed the experiment the results were statistically significant—the increase in creativity wasn't just down to chance). However you probably wouldn't notice the difference yourself, and if you did, you wouldn't attribute it to the different environment.

To be productive a creative environment should:

- be set up in a way that helps us implement projects (not follow systems or respond to stimulus)

- reflect the state we want our brain to be in—our thinking is more ordered in an ordered environment, and more cluttered in a cluttered environment.

For example, an aikido *dojo* (roughly translated as place of training) is conducive to training. It has only what is needed to develop one's practice. There are no distractions, and no extraneous ornaments. Likewise, work environments should be designed to be conducive to work.

Tools are also part of your environment. We all spend too little time getting good at using our tools, and too little time working on our environment. If you are a knowledge worker and your primary tool is your computer, invest time in mastering its use.

It's also worth noticing anything in your environment that takes your energy away—we want our environment to energise us. A friend of mine had a trophy of a past sporting victory in his office. But he had since had a falling out with the person he had won the trophy with. So rather than being a source of pride whenever he looked at the trophy, it drained his energy just a little. When he told me that, I took the trophy down and put it away in storage. He probably won't notice the difference, but I am sure at some level it will have an impact on how he feels, and consequently on his output.

Years ago I was working with a good friend, Ivan, who was doing some personal training with me. One of the first things he did was to take me shopping for training clothes. It seemed a bit strange at the time, but it was a smart move. It was part of my environment. When I was going to train, I put on my training clothes—the right costume for the right occasion. Even when I didn't feel like training, I knew that once I put my gear on, I would automatically take the next step. It became a trigger, and I knew I just had to get started by getting into my gear.

The lesson is to take your environment more seriously than you do now. If your workspace was a dojo for implementing great projects, how would you set it up, and what would you wear to maximise your productivity for the task?

Josh Kaufman, author of *The Personal MBA*, believes that for him the most important part of writing a best-selling book was establishing it as a project, and creating the environment for success. He says:

> I decided this is something I'm going to do. This is something I'm going to spend my time on versus other things...and just making some very simple interventions. So that was the summer that I cut my cable and got rid of my TV. Instead of watching movies or watching TV, or even taking a couple of months and going on vacation, I decided that I was just going to read a whole bunch of books.

> The wonderful part about publishing as it exists right now is it's very easy to put up a website, and it's very easy if you take just a little time every day to write about what you're doing or what you're learning. Part of the accountability I found for me was learning something really cool and then being able to share it with other people who appreciated it just as much as I did. So the website itself became a structure and became an accountability part of the project. This is seven going on eight years later and I still feel accountable to my readers to come back every single year with the results of my research on the best books that they can use to learn more about business. And best of all, I learned a ton in the process.

Method: how

Often we fail at projects simply because we don't know how to go about them. We don't know the steps to take. At the very least we need to know the next step.

Don't reinvent the wheel. Chances are your project is the same as or similar to something that has been done well. Do some research and choose the most appropriate methodology to fulfil your project. If your project is the same as something that's been done lots of times (for example, build a website, lose weight, write a book, fill a seminar), research the different methodologies and choose the one that fits best.

If you are doing something that hasn't been done before, or not done in your circumstances, determine if what you are doing is similar to existing projects. If so, find the appropriate methodologies and look to where you can combine them to create something new.

Of course, while you are following an existing methodology, don't assume it can't be done better. Refine along the way, and then, if appropriate, publish your improved version to the world.

Game

At the intersection of context and environment is game (see figure 5.1, p. 62). The more the project feels like a game, and the more it has the energy of play, the more likely it is to succeed.

Almost two decades ago I heard a story that has stuck with me ever since. It was about two boys catching a bus to school. Each morning they would mark a certain distance back from the bus stop and would wait at that mark until the bus came into sight. As soon as they saw the bus, the race was on. It was them versus the bus in a race to the bus stop, and they played like kids—the stakes were high. If they won, they were the champions of the world, and they would walk down the aisle to their seats arms aloft, as befitting world champions. If they lost—remember the stakes were high—they died. They would fall down dead on the footpath. And then get on the bus and go to school.

This is very different to how we usually play as adults. First, we almost never play full out. We're not treating the game like it's life or death, and giving it everything we have. We're playing it a bit safe, and keeping something in reserve. This is safer, because then, if we lose, we know that we didn't give it everything. We can say to ourselves: 'I wasn't really trying that hard, it doesn't mean I'm a failure, if I really wanted to I could have given more.'

Second, when we do lose, we don't just die, then get on the bus and go to school. We don't say to ourselves cool, lost that game, now what's the next game? We make it mean something about ourselves: 'I'm a failure', 'I'm not good enough', 'People will think less of me', and so on. Instead of simply recognising that game as one of the 50 per cent that we were supposed to lose, or one of the 1000 ways not to reinvent a light bulb and moving onto the next one, we take it personally. We get disempowered.

My good friend Jason Fox is a thought leader in combining behavioural science and game design to help people get stuff done and make stuff happen. He has written a great book called *Game On* about using games to execute ideas and accelerate innovation. Jason says:

Most roleplaying games (even before computers) involve people choosing 'characters' they want to make and play as. You might want to be a warrior hero, or a sorceress. In any event, you've got your character…but the only way that your character can grow and do cooler things is if you collect experience points. And the only way to get experience points in almost every roleplaying game (and heck, life itself) is by engaging in challenging work. These games create a natural bias to action by awarding points for anything that takes your character outside of their comfort zone.

We want to bring this energy to our projects. Play full out when the game is on, and be completely okay with failing a project, falling down dead, and moving on to the next game.

Progress

As figure 5.1 (p. 62) shows, at the intersection of context and method lies progress. As we will see in the team section of this book (part II), recent research shows us that of all the motivators, progress is the most powerful.

An interesting question to ask is whether it's more powerful to give feedback on progress in terms of progress that we have made, or what's left to go. In other words, if we were running a marathon, is it better to say we've run 10 km, or that we have 32 km to go?

In February 2012 the *Chicago Journals of Consumer Research* reported a study by Minjung Koo and Ayelet Fishbach, from the University of Chicago, that tested this exact question. The study was called 'The small-area hypothesis: effects of progress monitoring and goal adherence'. The authors found that, basically, we are more motivated by the part of our progress that is smaller in size, regardless of whether it represents accumulated progress or remaining progress.

In other words, for the first half of the marathon it's better to talk about how far we have run, but for the second half it's better to talk about how far there is still to go. I think this is fascinating, and very informative for how we motivate ourselves and our teams.

Because we are not wired for long-term projects, we need to build in short-term wins — an experience of progress that gives us pleasure in the short term — and know when to shift our focus from progress completed to future progress.

Good game design includes an experience of making progress. Likewise, part of your framework should be distinguishing and celebrating progress along the way. If you are like me and you have trouble completing the last 5 per cent then, according to this study, by focusing on only the remaining work to be done rather than on the 95 per cent completed, you increase your chances of completing.

Understanding how you work is critical to implementing important projects. Writing a book will give me a great deal of pleasure once it's done, but that could be a year away. That pleasure doesn't have much weight in my decision making today. I need to create motivation before then. I need a hit before then, both of pleasure if I make progress on the project, and pain if I don't. This is why milestones are so critical. This book is 55 000 words, but I had a lot of milestones along the way, with dates against them. I felt good when I hit them, and bad when I didn't. It's one of the ways I stay on track with my important projects.

Vision

Vision sits at the intersection of context and method, and connects your why with your how. The vision for a project is a picture of the project upon completion. What does the picture of success for the project look like?

One the habits Stephen Covey reports in *The 7 Habits of Highly Effective People* is 'start with the end in mind'. He says that every project, and every endeavour, is created twice: first in our imagination, and then in the world.

My friend Matt Church is a prolific writer and best-selling author with a dozen books to his name. He does something very interesting whenever he is starting a new book. He designs the cover, then prints and displays it. The vision for the project of writing a book is obviously a completed book (and apologies for using a book example again—understandably, it's on my mind at the moment). For Matt, the image of the cover is a great representation of this vision.

Our vision for a project is the first of these creations. It is useful to create a clear vision of what you are trying to create—the more detailed the better.

IN SUMMARY

Often projects fail because the framework we created was insufficient. The context for the project wasn't something that we were really aligned with. The vision wasn't sufficiently clear. We didn't create the right environment to complete the project in. Or perhaps we just didn't know how to go about it — our methodology was weak.

The danger is that we fail because of the framework, but our internal dialogue will tell us that we failed because we weren't good enough. We were not disciplined enough, or not committed enough, or not smart enough (or whatever our favourite flavour of 'not good enough' is).

Mostly we underestimate the power and impact of the framework on our implementation. It deserves more attention than most of us give it.

Three things to do

1   For the three projects that matter, clarify the purpose. Write down your big why, and make sure it's authentic. Is it something that you really want?

2   Create something in your environment to support the three projects — such as a display, a scoreboard or a dedicated space. Even a sticky note with the three projects on it somewhere prominent to remind you of the projects you are fighting for.

3   Spend at least 10 minutes on each of your three projects researching the best methodology to achieve the outcome you are looking for.

Chapter 6

SUPPORT

Keep away from people who try to belittle your ambitions.
Small people always do that, but the really great make you
feel that you, too, can become great.

Mark Twain, author

Implementation is a lot like sex. It's much harder on your own, and not nearly as much fun. To get anything significant done you need support—people to have your back and to have your front, people to walk the walk and to talk the talk.

Have your back

You want people who 'have your back' supporting your project (see figure 6.1, overleaf). My favourite example of someone having your back comes from Viking mythology. The Viking berserkers were Norse warriors who wore a bear-hide shirt (ber = bear, serk = shirt, therefore ber-serk = bear shirt). Old Norse literature reports berserkers would fight with 'a nearly uncontrollable trance-like fury', showing no regard for their own safety. Almost as important as the berserker was the guy who had the berserker's back. His role in battle wasn't to kill the enemy (the berserker was doing that just fine) but to have the berserker's back—to ensure that no-one killed the berserker from behind. This combination was so successful that just the appearance of Viking warriors wearing bear-shirts could make an army turn and run.

Figure 6.1: personal support model

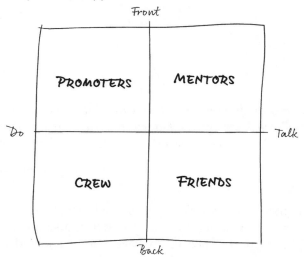

One of the functions of your supporters is to have your back. They fill in the pieces as you forge ahead, and support you from behind. They believe in you, and back you. As we can see in the model in figure 6.1, some of the people who have our back will be talking, cheering us on. Some will be doers, rolling up their sleeves and getting actively involved in the project.

Have your front

Equally you want people who 'have your front' supporting you. You want scouts in front who are determining what the terrain looks like.

In the Middle Ages, if you were someone of importance, you needed a couple of people to precede you when you were travelling—they had your front. First, you would want a guide who had travelled the path before and who knew the way—someone who could make sure you actually arrived at the place you wanted to get to (no GPS back then). Second, you couldn't send a text saying you were about to arrive, so you had a herald who would be out in front announcing that you were coming, preparing the way for your arrival and ensuring a warm welcome.

Do you have supporters who have your front? People who have been there and done that, and can show you the way? Do you have people who are announcing you, letting the world know that you are coming? Again, as we can see in the personal support model, some of our supporters out front are talkers, and some are doers. And we need both.

Talking

One half of the model in figure 6.1 is all about talking the talk. During all three phases of a project you need people to talk to. At the start, it might be about making sure that it's the right project and you are going about it the right way. During the persevere phase the talk could be about keeping you on track, and maintaining your belief. At the completing phase, the talk could be about making sure you cross the finish line, dealing with any final obstacles to publishing, and working out what's next.

Make sure you have the right people to talk to among your supporters. These people aren't there to actually roll up their sleeves and get their hands dirty, but that is not to say their role is any less important. The advisers to the prime minister don't carry out any of her commands, implement any of her projects, or help get tasks crossed off her to-do list. But their role is obviously critical, and the people who talk the talk are equally critical.

Doing

As important as the talking is, you want to be more than talk. You, and your team, need to also *walk* the talk. A critical part of being more productive is having supporters helping you do the doing. The left half of the model in figure 6.1 (p. 74) is all about the doing. This is where the rubber hits the road, and stuff actually happens.

Consequently there are four quadrants to the model and four critical roles for your supporters: mentors, friends, crew and promoters.

Mentors

Your mentors are the people who can accelerate your journey, and they are often people who have relevant experience.

About 15 years ago, when I was in my early twenties, I organised a bike ride to raise money for the Hunger Project, a charity that aims to end hunger on the planet. I was trying to get sponsorship for the event, and met up with a woman who had a consultancy connecting corporations and foundations with charities and causes where there was a good fit. I was very impressed by her — she had gone from a successful corporate career that was burning her out to creating the job of her dreams, using her skills to do great stuff and still getting well paid. I can't remember her name, and I never spoke with her again. She also didn't help me raise any money for our bike ride. However, she told me about something that had changed her life, and ultimately changed mine.

She told me that throughout her life she had always had mentors playing an important role in whatever she was up to. I decided then that I was going to do the same.

The following day I caught up with Suzanna, a nurse I had met recently, who sprang to mind when we talked about mentors. I asked Suzanna if she would be my mentor. She was a bit surprised: we didn't know each other very well, and we were in very different professions—she was a senior registered nurse; I was a management consultant at the time. She asked me why I wanted her as a mentor. I told her I wasn't sure: she had just come to mind when I was thinking about a mentor, and I trusted my intuition. She then asked what being a mentor meant. I said I wasn't sure about that either. With that brief, Suzanna accepted, and became the first of many important mentors in my life.

Suzanna went on to become a very important figure in my life, and she has consistently helped me to step back from whatever I am doing and ask why am I doing it? What's the bigger picture here? My intuition proved right—she was the perfect mentor for me at the time.

Since then I have actively sought mentors in all the important domains and the important projects in my life. I have mentors around my health, fitness, money, relationships and, of course, in the different aspects of my practice and my businesses.

Mentors have three roles in your projects:

- *Positioning and leverage.* I wrote my first book, *Sell Your Thoughts*, with Matt Church and Scott Stein. Matt, who has been a mentor of mine for a number of years, is Australia's premier keynote speaker, and also the founder of Thought Leaders Global. By co-authoring a book with him I was leveraging off his position in the market, and as a result my personal brand grew by association. So one type of mentor to look for is one who can provide positioning and leverage for you. Matt has actually fulfilled the next two functions for me as well.

- *Skills and capability*. When I mentor a client around commercialising their expertise, I primarily provide skills and capabilities. One objective of the mentoring is to help them develop their ability to effectively set up and conduct sales meetings. So typically we might review a phone call or a meeting that they had recently held, and look at what they could do better next time. Or we might identify which skills they need to improve.

- *Strategy and direction*. When I work with business owners this is mostly where we work. We talk about the vision for their business, the strategy to get there, and what will be the best path forward for them.

I recently spoke with somebody who was looking for a mentor for a business she was launching in Australia. It was a very specific niche within public relations — talent procurement. It was an industry I had never really thought about. If you have an event or a marketing campaign and you want a particular celebrity or 'talent' to represent you, how do you get hold of them? That's what a talent procurement agency is all about.

I had been recommended as a business mentor, and we had a coffee and a chat about what she wanted to do and what she needed. I could have provided general business skills and capabilities, and also strategy and direction, but what she really needed was positioning and leverage. She needed someone with connections and a presence in the industry to help position her and connect her, and to help her launch. I told her right then that I wasn't the right person to mentor her.

As I said, sometimes a mentor will fulfil all three functions, and sometimes they provide one or two. Aaron is my mentor in the domain of my health and fitness. He helps me train, work out my diet, and so on. He works with me primarily in the skills and capability function. He teaches me what exercises will do what, and how to do them properly. In that domain, that's all I want. I don't need positioning or leverage around my fitness, and I'm already pretty clear on the direction and strategy. What I'm looking for from Aaron is for him to help me develop my skills and capability.

When you are looking for a mentor it is extremely useful to identify which function or functions you are looking for. It is also worth considering the existing mentors in your life, and seeing where they sit.

Friends

Within your support structure, your friends are the people who keep you true to who you are and what you do.

They are the people you can talk to when you need some support to keep going, or if you need clarity about what's going on. A friend in this context is different from a purely social friend: it is a friend who is supporting you as you implement your important projects. I have some friends who I might go to the footy with, or catch up with at a party or for a drink when they are in town. These are people I enjoy spending time with, or relaxing with and having a laugh. These aren't the friends I'm talking about here.

The friends in the context of a project are people you can go to for counsel, whom you can talk to when you're struggling. They are also people you can count on for honest feedback. My wife, Trish, has this role in most of my important projects. I know she believes in me 100 per cent, and that perspective is great when I doubt myself. At the same time, she will always be direct, and if I'm making a mistake or doing something dumb, she will tell me.

Crew

Crew are the people you can rely on to make stuff happen. This is what you might call your core team or, in some instances your staff. These are the people who do most of the doing, and they definitely have your back.

My business manager, Cristina, is the key member of my crew. In most of my projects and my businesses I can tell her what I want to happen, and she will make it happen.

With some personal projects, there might not be anyone in this role: in some cases it's all up to you.

Promoters

Promoters create positive noise around your projects; they let the world know what you are up to. Again, some projects won't need this, but if you are up to big stuff, there are definitely times you need support promoting what you do in the world.

When I organised the Hunger Project bike ride, which ran over three years (I should clarify that it was once a year for three years—we didn't ride for three years solid), we raised $50 000. Some members of the team didn't ride: they were solely promoters—their role was to tell people about the ride and get them along.

——————— IN SUMMARY ———————

For many projects support is the critical success factor: you can't implement most great projects on your own.

Some projects will just need one support person in one of the four quadrants. Sometimes one person will fulfil roles in multiple quadrants. Sometimes a project will justify having support people in all four domains.

At the start of a project determine if this is something you can do on your own, or if you want support. Then determine the types of supporters you need, and which people you want to enrol to be part of the project. Bring your own tribe together with the right people in the right support roles to ensure your project receives the support it needs to be successful.

Three things to do

1   For an important project in your world, write down everyone you would love to have supporting you to make it happen.

2   Identify which of the four roles (mentor, friend, crew, promoter) you want each person to fulfil.

3   Have a conversation with all the people on your list and invite them to be part of the project.

Chapter 7

– ACCOUNTABILITY –

*Part of the accountability I found for me was learning
something really cool and then being able to share it with
other people who appreciated it just as much as I did.*

Josh Kaufman, author of *The Personal MBA*

Keeping any long-term project alive requires accountability.
We are not wired to achieve long-term goals: instead, we
have evolved over hundreds of thousands of years to survive
immediate threats. It's what our neurology, biochemistry and
instincts are hardwired for. Long-term projects require that we
defer gratification, but we are biologically set up to take the
actions that give us pleasure or help us avoid pain in the short
term. It's why big projects are so difficult, and why we need to
be accountable to persevere.

A famous experiment was conducted in 1972 by psychologist
Walter Mischel of Stanford University—the now famous
Stanford Marshmallow Experiment. In the study, a marshmallow

was offered to each child in the study group of preschoolers. If the child could resist eating the marshmallow for 15 minutes, they were promised two instead of one. The scientists analysed how long each child resisted the temptation to eat the marshmallow, and whether doing so had any correlation with their future success. The results provided researchers with great insight into the psychology of self-control.

While a few children ate the marshmallow immediately, of the more than 600 who took part in the experiment, one-third could defer gratification long enough to get the second marshmallow. The experiment confirmed the hypothesis that age does determine the development of deferred gratification: older children were generally able to hold out for longer.

However, it was the follow-up study 18 years later that made the experiment famous. It found that the ability of the children to defer gratification had a strong correlation with higher SAT (college entrance) scores. In other words, the kids who could hold out the 15 minutes for the second marshmallow were the ones that performed better in high school and college. In fact, the ability to defer gratification at preschool age had a higher correlation with future success than socioeconomic factors, family structure or any other factor considered!

Since we have evolved to survive, and to move towards pleasure and away from pain, that generally means we feel pleasure about the things that will help us and the species survive (such as eating when we're hungry, drinking when we're thirsty, staying warm, having sex), and we experience pain with things that would generally hurt our chances of survival (such as being rejected by our tribe, feeling hungry or cold, or having a broken leg).

Sigmund Freud, the father of modern psychology, observed that everything that we do is either a move towards pleasure or away from pain, and he called this the pleasure principle.

The problem is our brain is not good at dealing with something that will give us pain now but pleasure later, or pleasure now but pain later. We are not good at making that calculation. Historically it wasn't something that we needed in order to survive.

Exercise is a great example of this. Getting up at 6 am on a cold winter morning to go exercise never feels as good as staying in a warm bed in the short term, but it will probably make you feel better in an hour's time, when you have finished. Consistently exercise, and accept the short-term pain for the long-term gain, and you will definitely feel better in 30 years' time than if you hadn't.

An opposite example is taking heroin. In the short term, by all accounts, there is very little on the planet that will make you feel better. There is plenty of evidence that there is also little on the planet that can make you feel worse over the longer term. Unfortunately, there are plenty of people who are willing to make this trade.

Think about where in your own life you are not good at making that calculation, of judging the short-term pain versus long-term pleasure, or the other way around.

Unfortunately, with most projects, the very things that will provide success and fulfilment require that we defer gratification. We need to learn to deal with some short-term pain for the longer-term benefit. This is where accountability comes in. It helps us do what we say we are going to do — remember, one of the essential elements in creating an implementation mindset is doing what you say.

As shown in figure 7.1, accountability can be to ourselves (private), to our peers, to someone in a position of authority (positional) or to the world at large (public). There are pros and cons at each level. With each project it makes sense to determine the most effective level of accountability.

Figure 7.1: accountability model

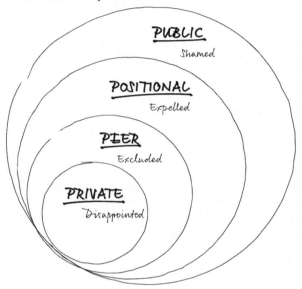

If you think back to our primary implementation model (see figure 2.1, p. 23), you will recall that accountability sits in the bottom left corner, helping us *execute* in *time*. This model unpacks the different levels of accountability from private right through to public, and how and when to use each one.

Private

Private accountability, that is, personal integrity, is our ability to keep promises to ourselves. This is the muscle that was tested in the marshmallow experiment—the ability to defer gratification. Personal integrity is tested by temptation: for instance, I have promised myself I will give up smoking, but I have just been offered a cigarette, and I really feel like having one *now*.

Private is the least powerful level of accountability. That is not to say it's not effective or not worth working on, but if a project is important and difficult, you shouldn't rely on private accountability to get it done.

If we don't keep our promises to ourselves, we will be disappointed in ourselves. Sometimes that isn't a strong enough motivator to overcome inertia, or resist the temptation of immediate gratification.

Peer

We have evolved to not let down our tribe—we don't want to let others down or look bad, and our default position is to do whatever we can to avoid this. This is why external accountability is effective. Peer accountability is the first level of this.

We all have, in certain areas of our life, a level of accountability to ourselves that is sufficient. But for most of us, most of the time, it is much safer and more effective to have an external accountability structure.

Imagine that you decide you are going to learn guitar over the next three months. You have bought a book on learning to play guitar and have decided you are going to practise four times a week. You have a very strong motivation for doing so—you really want to be able to play the guitar, you have friends that you could jam with, and perhaps you could even join a band. Together, these are some pretty good reasons to stick to your plan, but you haven't tapped into one of the most powerful motivators, because you haven't told anyone else about your project: it's just you.

Now, imagine that you set up an external accountability structure. You get two buddies to buy guitars and learn with you. You decide to practise together four times a week. Now, insane as it sounds, not letting down your two buddies is a better motivation than all your own reasons for wanting to learn guitar. This is because at a primal level we are tribal creatures. We don't want to be excluded from the tribe, so the motivation to not let down our peers is stronger at a deep emotional level than the motivation to not disappoint ourselves.

So set up as many peer accountability structures as you can to keep you true to your path.

Positional

Positional accountability is more powerful again—the drive to not let down someone that we respect in a position of power or authority. Again this is very primal. Historically our survival was linked to the survival of the group, and the chief was responsible for the whole tribe. The ultimate punishment was being expelled from the tribe, and we have a primal fear of this, which can kick in when we choose to be accountable to someone in a position of power.

Of course, it is also up to us who we give positional authority. When we were young it was probably our parents, teachers and coaches. Today, equally, it may be our boss, or someone with authority in our workplace.

Positional authority ups the ante. The potential reward or punishment, real or perceived, is greater. As a kid, the stakes are different when a project is due to be handed in to your teacher than they are when you have agreed with your friends to do something fun. Likewise, something that your parents are expecting has a different weight to something you are doing with your siblings.

To understand this at a more individual level, let's use an example. When you take on a guitar teacher you are granting them positional authority to hold you accountable. Because they are being paid, and because they are an expert, we grant them positional authority. Using a teacher as part of an accountability structure to learn guitar is more powerful again for most people than setting up a structure with our buddies.

Public

Public accountability is even more powerful. If everyone in our world knows about a project that we are committed to, it makes it even harder for us to back out of it.

In 2010 I did a two-day program run by Matt Church. Matt has since become my mentor, business partner and great friend, but that was the first time we had done anything together. The program was called Million Dollar Expert, and it was about commercialising thought leadership as an infopreneur: a subject matter expert working on their own. It was the best professional development I had ever done, and I was excited about implementing it in my own work.

Of course, I created a project—and I wanted the project to be a stretch. I set the goal of going from what Matt Church called *white belt* (earning $10000 a month) to *black belt* (earning $60000 a month) in my practice within a year. This was a pretty important project, and one that was going to be pretty challenging, so I chose the public level of accountability. I figured I would need all the help I could get.

I did this by creating a blog—'White Belt to Black Belt in 365 Days'—and committed to updating it every week with my progress. I could have made the decision myself and kept it private by not telling anyone. Or I could have told my wife, or the other participants of the course, and put the project at the peer level. Alternatively, I could have told Matt, and made it positional. But making it public was more powerful than any of those options.

I ended up having my first black-belt month 125 days later, and my practice has been at or above that level ever since. (The blog of that journey is compiled into an e-book that you can download from the freebies page of my website— www.petercook.com.)

IN SUMMARY

The skill you need for accountability is to pick the most effective level of accountability for each project.

Lots of projects will live in the private sphere. With my aikido training, my current project is to get my third dan by the age of 40. My training is now so habitual, I've been happy to have private accountability in that project. If I had a buddy I always trained with, that would be peer accountability.

Some projects are worth using positional authority. I have mentors in lots of domains of my life—my health and wellbeing, my money, my businesses and more. These mentors are witnesses for the projects that are the most important in each of these domains—I have given them positional authority.

Finally, there are times where the most effective accountability will be public—for the projects that are important enough and big enough to justify it.

Three things to do

1 For each of the projects in your portfolio write down the current accountability level. (If you are thinking there isn't an accountability, it means the accountability is personal.)

2 Determine which projects do not have the optimal accountability level (mostly it will be too low).

3 Where it makes sense to increase the accountability level, create a higher accountability structure that makes sense to you.

PART II

TEAM

Chapter 8
TEAM
——— OVERVIEW ———

*People are always blaming their circumstances for
what they are. I don't believe in circumstances.
The people who get on in this world are the people
who get up and look for the circumstances they want,
and, if they can't find them, make them.*

George Bernard Shaw, playwright

Traditional management practices have come out of the industrial revolution and are based on an assembly line model. People are effectively treated as cogs in the machine, and motivated with a carrot and stick approach.

Historically, Economics 101 taught us that more money was the ultimate motivator. If you wanted people to work harder, then you should pay them more. However some amazing research over the last decade has looked at what motivates us, and has disproved this theory. For anything more than mechanical, repetitive work, after a certain point money actually acts as a disincentive. You need to pay people enough to take the issue of payment off the table, because naturally people will be disgruntled and leave if they are getting paid less than their market worth. Beyond that, however, the science shows us that money doesn't act as a motivator.

American journalist and speechwriter Daniel H. Pink writes in *Drive: The Surprising Truth About What Motivates Us*, that thinking money is the number one motivator is a mistake: 'The secret to high performance and satisfaction—at work, at school, and at home—is the deeply human need to direct our own lives, to learn and create new things, and to do better by ourselves and our world.'

Pink draws on four decades of research on human motivation to expose the mismatch between what science has discovered and how businesses behave. He emphasises that while carrots and sticks may have worked during the industrial revolution, it's absolutely the wrong way to motivate people to perform today. In *Drive*, he examines the three elements of true motivation:

- autonomy

- mastery

- purpose.

Pink offers smart and surprising techniques for putting these elements into action. Along the way, he reveals the practices of companies using these new approaches to motivation and introduces the scientists and entrepreneurs leading the way. Let's have a look at the power of each of these elements.

Not surprisingly, adults like to have a degree of autonomy. We like to be trusted. Years of hanging out with my nephews have taught me that kids like the same thing, and that conversely, it is demotivating to be told exactly what to do all the time.

We are also motivated by mastery: the opportunity to better ourselves, to make progress. My wife Trish loves skiing, and she skis beautifully. While I basically fall down the mountain narrowly avoiding disaster at every turn, Trish gracefully glides down the slopes. There is a lot that Trish loves about skiing: just being up in the mountains, the feeling of a good turn, the rush of speed, the challenge and the exercise. The thing she loves most is getting better: the knowledge at the end of the week that she is better than she was at the start of the week, that she has moved one step closer to mastery. And the science shows that she is not alone in this. Within the workplace a key motivator is the opportunity to be challenged and to improve ourselves.

Finally, there is purpose: the experience of making a difference for the greater good with what we do. While companies have an obligation to aim to make money for their owners, increasing shareholder value is rarely a sufficient purpose to motivate us to jump out of bed and race into work every morning.

The new rules of management require that we provide our teams with all three of these components: autonomy, mastery and purpose.

There is no better way to achieve that than implementing projects that matter. If you want motivated, engaged, switched-on people performing at their peak, the science tells us to give them work that stretches them and means something, and then get out of their way. Don't take them on a team-building retreat; don't put them on a high ropes course or give them another set of core values — give them projects that matter, and leave them to it. Magic lives in these projects. They are the key to having teams that rock.

Managing a team is a great responsibility. If fulfilment comes from doing great work, and you lead a team, you have the opportunity to either have team members going home spent, having given their all for a shared purpose they believe in; or you are sucking their souls dry, requiring them to use only a fraction of themselves and live for the weekend.

What's at stake is the difference between the potential results and the actual results. The majority of teams use only a

TEAM

fraction of the talent, skills and spirit of their members. And consequently, they achieve only a fraction of their potential. As the manager of a team you either provide your team the opportunity to do great work — or you don't. I believe this is sacred work, and that the ultimate measure of how well you lead or manage a team is the gap between the potential of the team members and what actually gets achieved.

Implementing projects that matter is the best way to do great work, to have the team engaged and fulfilled, and to achieve the best results. And this is the management imperative of the 21st century.

Within our teams, as we can see from the primary implementation model shown again in figure 8.1, there are a number of different elements in creating and executing projects.

Figure 8.1: primary implementation model

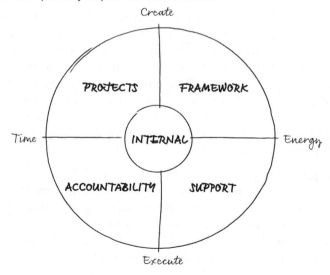

Internal

The internal element is the culture of the team. Often teams have a culture that stymies the implementation of projects that matter: they may be risk-averse, political or just plain uninspiring. Important projects are challenging enough even with a strong culture—a weak culture will make them virtually impossible.

A high-performance culture is one that empowers the team to create and execute projects that matter. The culture is demonstrated through the different phases of a project: the beginning, the middle and the end. The culture reveals itself in the energy of the team, what they do and what they say.

Projects

As we saw earlier, as individuals we have five possible behaviours—instincts, responses, habits, systems and projects. In our teams the first one drops off, leaving us with responses, habits, systems and projects. No matter what level we look at—individual, team or organisation—projects demand the most of us, but they are where we get the biggest payoffs.

A team's core business is rooted in the responses, habits and systems that the team follows. These are all important, and these are what pay the bills. The more efficiently projects are done, the better. The projects that matter are those where new stuff gets created and where innovation lives. Projects are what make a team inspiring to be a part of.

Framework

The framework within which our teams implement projects is made up of the context, the environment and the method. The framework answers the questions why we implement, how we do it, and where.

Within the team domain the essential characteristic of our framework is that it is shared. It is critical that the team is aligned to the why, where and how of the major projects. Too often the manager holds the context for a project, but it isn't powerfully shared with the team.

Support

Part of prioritising projects within our teams is providing the necessary support. Four key roles support the team to implement projects:

- *Advisers* are the people who help the team figure out what's next; they are often people outside the team who have experience in the relevant domain.

- *Buddies* are people to talk to when the going gets tough, often peers outside the core project team who can act as a sounding board and a support structure, particularly during the middle phase of a project, when it's necessary to persevere and it's often tempting to abandon a project.

- *Assistants* help with the background tasks to free up the team. They are another great support structure to help get projects implemented.

- *Champions* are the external people who will go into bat for the team and the project.

Accountability

A good accountability structure is a critical component of implementing projects that matter. Projects take effort, and we usually come to a point when it seems harder to go on, and suddenly abandoning this project for a new, shiny one seems like a good idea. This is why we need the right level of accountability—to help us push through.

Accountability can exist at four different levels: private, positional, peer and public. The stakes rise through these accountability levels. If we pull out, personal accountability makes us disappointed with ourselves—but only with ourselves. When we are accountable to a peer, there is a primal fear not only of disappointing ourselves, but also of being excluded from the tribe. When we are accountable to someone in a position of authority, the fear rises to that of being expelled from the tribe. The greatest accountability is to the public—everyone outside our team—where the stakes are highest.

TEAM

Chapter 9

INTERNAL

——————— CULTURE ———————

In order to succeed, you must first be willing to fail.

Anonymous

Culture can be understood basically as 'how things are done around here'. While an organisation as a whole has its own culture or climate when it comes to implementing projects that matter (which we will come to in part III on organisations), each team has its own culture too.

Many teams have a culture that impedes the implementation of projects that matter. The culture may be risk-averse, so it feels dangerous to try something new. A team may be in survival mode, struggling to do the current work with no space for new projects. The culture may be political, where team members are competing with each other, rather than working together. Or the team culture may just be uninspired—just going through the motions. Any of these problems in a team will make it very difficult for them to implement new projects. Projects are challenging enough even with a strong culture, so a weak culture will make implementation almost impossible.

A high-performance culture is one that empowers the team to do the work that matters. Michael Henderson, known as the Corporate Anthropologist, a true thought leader and a good friend of mine, wrote about the three elements of a high-performance culture in a blog post entitled 'The 3 basics of developing high performance cultures at work' (www. culturesatwork.com/blog-michael-henderson):

> In all the observations and work I've done with organisational culture over the last 20 years, I've come to believe that there are three basic requirements for a culture to be strong and sustainable. These are having Leaders Worth Following, developing a workplace Culture Worth Belonging To and people experiencing Work Worth Doing.
>
> ### A leader worth following
>
> A leader worth following is one who embodies the ideals and values of the tribe's culture. A leader who is able and willing to tell the tribe's stories regularly and with conviction, thus enabling the people to be reminded who they are. A leader worth following takes a deep and ongoing interest in the wellbeing of the people. The leader knows the culture, and sees culture as the key to weaving the people together.
>
> ### A culture worth belonging to
>
> A culture worth belonging to, is a culture where people feel a part of something that enriches their lives, and adds to their personal sense of identity. A culture worth belonging to, is typically deeply meaningful, and symbolically represents something greater than the individuals can attain or experience alone. A culture worth belonging to, is a leader's primary responsibility. Without it, the tribe's days are numbered.
>
> ### Work worth doing
>
> No one likes to experience meaningless or soul destroying work. A leader must consider and truly understand why the work the organisation is engaged in is actually worth doing in the first place. The leader must have great clarity and a sense of purpose about the work and be able to explain to and remind people of this purpose. We are in the 21st Century and, unlike

the many generations that came before us, we have choices about how and where we earn a living. Meaningless work for increasing numbers of people is no longer acceptable. In reality, the meaning of work is, for many employees, now regarded as their second pay slip.

To develop and maintain high performing cultures, leaders must deliberately and incessantly ensure these three factors, Leaders Worth Following, Cultures Worth Belonging To and Work Worth Doing, are a daily reality within the organisation.

I think Michael is bang on the money, and that while these three elements sound quite simple, they are profound. I think that the key to all of them is the creation and execution of projects that matter.

This starts with work worth doing. A team comes together to achieve or produce something, to do the work of the team. Projects that matter make that team worth belonging to.

A culture worth belonging to is one that allows this work to occur, and results in team members feeling proud of their contribution.

Finally, a leader worth following is someone inspires and unites the team. The best way to do that is through the work itself, by bringing the team together in service of the work worth doing (that is, projects that matter), and having the team inspired by what they are pouring their life energy into.

Culture—the way things are done around here—includes the energy of the team, what they do and what they say.

As we saw in part I, every project goes through three distinct phases: the beginning, the middle and the end. And obviously these make up the start, persevere and complete phases of the implementation culture model. As we can see in the model in figure 9.1 (overleaf), six key elements to an implementation culture support our project through these three phases.

TEAM

Figure 9.1: implementation culture model

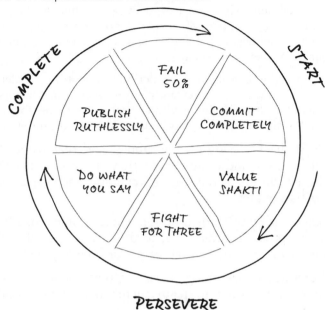

Fail 50 per cent

In any given project or endeavour, we can succeed or fail, and we can go about every project flat-out or half-hearted, which give us four options:

- *Succeeding half-hearted.* Some things we can only put a bit of ourselves into and still pull off. Nice when you do that, but generally this attitude is not going to be enough for pulling off the big things.

- *Succeeding flat-out.* These are the things that give us the greatest satisfaction—we have left nothing in the tank, and come out victorious.

- *Failing half-hearted.* This is playing safe. We can fool ourselves into thinking we didn't really fail because we didn't give it everything. Too much of this kind of behaviour is dangerous — we can get in the habit of failing without being responsible for the failure, and the habit of not giving our best.

- *Failing flat-out.* This can be the hardest, and it is by far the most important. All successful people and teams have had spectacular failures giving their all. It is the most important because without being willing to fail flat-out, we'll never succeed flat-out.

Failing flat-out is what we need to become comfortable with, and why I recommend that people aim to fail 50 per cent of the time. This applies to our innovative projects, not to everything we do. In the next chapter, we will come back to the distinction between responses, systems and projects. When responding to direct instructions or requests, or following systems, we generally want to get it right. So be a bit selective about when to apply the fail 50 per cent rule. Please don't tell the police officer who has pulled you over that Pete said fail 50 per cent and so now you only stop at every second red light.

In the right areas, allowing ourselves to fail 50 per cent of the time lets us risk failing flat-out. If we aren't able to risk failing at 100 per cent effort, then we will be half-hearted in everything we do, and we will never succeed flat-out either.

In *Bull Durham*, one of my favourite movies, Tim Robbins's character 'Nuke' La Loosh is in the middle of a winning streak when he says something very profound about success and failure: 'I love winning...you know...it's like better than losing.' Emotionally he's right, but in terms of building character and learning about yourself, failing flat-out beats winning every time.

So go out and fail, fail hard, fail often, fail spectacularly, fail at the right things and fail flat-out — 50 per cent of the time.

TEAM

Commit completely

As we have seen, every project goes through three phases: start, persevere and complete. At the start, we need to commit completely to our projects. My favourite quote in the whole world encapsulates this. Scottish mountaineer W. H. Murray said:

> Until one is committed, there is hesitancy, the chance to draw back, always ineffectiveness...The moment one definitely commits oneself, then providence moves too. All sorts of things occur to help one that would never otherwise have occurred. A whole stream of events issue from the decision, raising in one's favour all manner of unforeseen incidents and meetings and material assistance, which no man could have dreamt would have come his way. I have learnt a great respect for one of Goethe's couplets: Whatever you can do, or dream you can, begin it. Boldness has genius and power and magic in it!

When a team is 100 per cent committed to a project, everything is different. The question changes from 'Can we do this?' to 'How will we do this?' Being interested in executing projects that matter isn't enough. It takes commitment. Being 100 per cent committed means being willing to do whatever it takes.

In my city, Melbourne, Australian Rules football is often compared to religion. I heard a commentator on television say that in his family it's known that if they don't barrack for Geelong (one of the Victorian teams) Santa won't come. Normally I would be horrified by such blatant manipulation, but I have to admit, when I heard that I tucked it away in the back of mind for future use.

We're an Essendon family. My daughter will be a fifth-generation Essendon supporter. My dad welcomed my wife Trish into the family by presenting her with an Essendon scarf. In 1999 Essendon was the best team; it finished on top of the ladder, and was favourite to win the grand final, but the week before the grand final, tragedy struck. We lost. Not only did we lose, we lost to our arch-enemy, Carlton. Not only did we lose to our arch-enemy, Carlton, we lost by one point! That day was possibly the low point of my life to date.

It wasn't a great day for the players either, I imagine. But that night the team gathered in the stands of the Melbourne Cricket Ground (the venue of the grand final) and launched the project to win the next year's grand final—no matter what it took.

Traditionally, the winning team sings its theme song after every game, but halfway through the following season, the Essendon players stopped singing after wins. They made a pact that they weren't going to sing the song again until the job was done. On that last Saturday in September 2000, after the most successful season in the history of the AFL, with only one loss throughout the year, and after the victory lap and the medals had been awarded, the Essendon Football team took the premiership cup to the centre circle of the Melbourne Cricket Ground. They formed a circle around the cup, and they sang the theme song for the first time in three months.

The project to win that grand final, launched in the aftermath of the previous year's loss, was a powerful one. There was no doubt that every member of the team had committed to it completely. No-one was only half in. No-one was waiting to see how it panned out. They were in 100 per cent, and they were going to do whatever it took. That's exactly what we want to do at the start of every project, and that's the sort of energy and intent we need to bring to our projects that matter.

Value shakti

What we do, particularly as we move into the persevere phase of a project, is all about managing energy, or as I prefer to term it, valuing shakti. As we saw earlier, shakti is a Sanskrit word that means more than energy—it's something like your life force, your spirit, your energy and your essence all rolled into one.

Implementing projects that matter takes shakti—you can't just show up and go through the motions.

The idea of valuing shakti builds on both time management and prioritisation, taking them both further. You definitely need to manage your time and clarify your priorities, but even more importantly, you need to value your life force or shakti.

In David Allen's seminal work, *Getting Things Done* (a book that I have given to many friends and clients), he recommends that, in deciding what to do, you consider, in the following order:

- *your context (where you are)*—obviously, what you can do standing in line in the supermarket is different from what you can do in your office
- *time*—how much time you have available
- *energy*—what your energy level is
- *importance*—how important the different tasks you need to complete are.

Valuing your shakti means taking into account your energy levels when considering how best to spend your time, as David Allen recommends. When you are switched on, don't waste time on trivial stuff. When your shakti is low, adjust accordingly, and knock of some of the easier things on your list.

However, shakti means much more than energy levels. Valuing shakti means recognising that your results are more a product of your team's shakti than of their time. Fifteen minutes of inspired thinking when they are completely switched on, energised, in tune with themselves and the world, and full of shakti can be infinitely more valuable than a day's work when they are exhausted, distracted, depressed or on autopilot.

Valuing shakti means allowing your team to do more of their best work more often, and doing what it takes to keep them in a state to be able to do that.

Fight for three

Your team can't put in 80 hours a week of significant, creative, real work. Unfortunately, time is much easier to measure than results, so mostly what we expect from people in our teams is that they 'do the time'. It's completely normal for someone to turn up to work on Monday morning a bit the worse for wear, feeling tired and sleep-deprived (and definitely not valuing shakti) after a big weekend. Surviving eight hours of work without really being present and without achieving anything worthwhile is not unusual.

Imagine, on the other hand, someone in your team coming to you at lunchtime and saying, 'I've had an amazing morning. I got in a bit early, and have produced these three breakthrough results on the project. I think I'll knock off now and head down to the beach'. It's unheard of—but, really, isn't that preferable to simply putting in the hours? By far?

When I worked at Accenture there were people who always came in early and left late. It was a badge of honour, and part of the culture of the organisation was to do long hours. And there was something seductive about it. Typically, on a project, when it got to 7 pm someone would organise dinner for the night, and a bunch of pizzas or Chinese food or something else would show up. There was something fun about it, and it became normal for a lot of people.

When you're in a work environment like that, Parkinson's law kicks in—the work will expand to fill the available time. If you are going to work until 10 pm, there is no urgency to get on

TEAM

111

with something now. And even if we wanted to, it's impossible to do great work for long stretches of time.

In part I, I wrote about fighting each day for three productive sessions of hard, creative, important work that produce a significant outcome. If you have taken on that practice, share it with your team, and encourage them to do the same.

I also talked about picking three professional projects each 90 days that I would fight for, and focus on. Again this is something that you can share with your team, and ask them to apply. Imagine if every quarter, every member of your team had three significant outcomes they were striving for, and they were implementing three projects that mattered to them. These might be sub-projects within a bigger project, professional development projects, sales or service related ... the possibilities are endless. And of course everyone should be setting the projects at a level where they expect to fail 50 per cent of them.

And finally, as a team, fight for three projects. At any time the whole team should be able to say that these are the three projects that we are focused on right now. There might be 15 other projects happening, and hundreds of systems being followed, and thousands of different inputs being responded to. But implementing three projects in a 90-day period that inspire the team, and that produce results that matter—that's worth fighting for.

Do what you say

One of the most critical elements of creating an implementation culture within a team is integrity—creating a culture where people do what they say. And the most important thing you can do to instil this in your team is to model it. Be a person of integrity yourself. If you say you are going to send out an email this afternoon, send it out. If you call a meeting at 10 am, be there at 10 am. Keep the promises you make to your clients, to your team and to everyone else in the organisation.

When you model integrity, you can then expect it from everyone else. Often this also means making communication tighter and cleaner. There are four elements of powerful communication that are worth playing with, and even mastering: requests, promises, declarations and acknowledgements.

A clean request is different from an order, and it is much more powerful. When you give an order, the other person doesn't have a choice. There are times when this is appropriate, when you have the authority to tell someone what to do, and you do. A request is different—it's when you ask somebody to do something. And the most powerful request is to take an action or produce a result by a particular time. For example 'Will you please complete this document and send it to me by 5 pm on Thursday?' There are four possible responses to a request:

- Accept: Yes I will.

- Decline: No, sorry, I won't.

- Counteroffer: I can't get it to you by Thursday, but I can by Friday.

- Postpone: I'm not sure—I'll look at what I have on, and let you know first thing tomorrow.

When you make a request cleanly, you leave room for all these responses. That's what distinguishes a request from an order—a request offers room for someone to decline.

A promise is a future-based commitment: 'I will take this action or produce this result by this time.' Again a promise is more powerful if a time is included: a 'what by when'.

A declaration is a description of how things are now. A set of core values is a declaration: this is how we operate. This is what you can count on. A powerful declaration doesn't just

TEAM

describe the world—it creates it. When you declare that you are a person of integrity, that you do what you say, that is more than a report based on the evidence. You are not saying that in the last year you have made 4035 promises and kept 3095 of them, so on balance you keep more promises than you break. You are creating the world in the present moment with yourself as a person of integrity. It's a big idea, and beyond the scope of the current discussion, but if you want to delve more deeply, Eckhart Tolle explores integrity in *The Power of Now*.

And finally, acknowledgement describes the past. Again, a powerful acknowledgement is creative and not just descriptive. Acknowledgement is much more powerful than we think. Carol Dweck, the Lewis and Virginia Eaton Professor of Psychology at Stanford University, has done some fascinating research into what she has termed the 'effort effect'. She found that praising children for intelligence rather then effort actually sapped their motivation. And while much of her research has been done on school children, the lessons have been applied to business, sports and interpersonal relationships. The lesson from her research is to acknowledge effort (the behaviour we want to reinforce) rather than something that is seen as a natural ability, like intelligence or creativity.

If you can introduce these elements of communication into your team, you'll go a long way towards creating a culture of integrity.

Publish ruthlessly

My brother Ben heads up an IT team at a finance company. Ben and his team have won a number of awards, and have produced the best online software in their industry. They have a mantra: 'We're not trying to put a man on the moon.'

If you are working at NASA, close enough is not good enough. When you are trying to put a person on the moon, everything has to be perfect. It's appropriate to obsess about every detail, check and double-check everything, test and retest each component, and take as long as you need to.

Most things we do aren't like that. I can write an article in 15 minutes or in an hour. As long as I have a decent idea to write about, the one-hour version won't be that much better than the 15-minute version. It's the law of diminishing returns. Whether it's worth pursuing those returns depends where the article is being published. If *The New York Times* commissioned me to write an article, I would spend a day on it, but for my blog, 15 minutes is generally enough.

The mistake that many of us make is that when we could have produced something good enough in 15 minutes, and had it out there, we decide we need an hour. Then, because we don't have an hour, it doesn't happen. Instead of having something good enough out in the world, we don't have anything.

Ben and his team have this down in spades. When a feature of their software actually manages the movement of money, then they know that is their equivalent of sending people to the moon, and they are going to get it right. But anything else — improvements to the user interface, new reports, additional features or tweaks that their customers have asked for — they produce quickly and publish. This focus on rapid publishing means that every four to six weeks something new gets added to the system. Their users love this. They love having the best product in the market; they love the responsiveness of the company to requests and suggestions; and they love that it keeps improving.

Every now and then, when there is a glitch or something doesn't work perfectly right off the bat, the customers are forgiving. They recognise how quickly the product is being developed, and new features are being added, and understand that means not everything will be perfect first time around.

TEAM

————— IN SUMMARY —————

One of the most important things you can do as the manager of a team is to create an implementation culture. A culture where there is a strong commitment to projects that matter as the highest priority within the team. A culture where failure is not only accepted, or even encouraged, but demanded. A culture where results are valued over time; and where stuff gets finished and published into the world. A culture that values shakti, where the manager focuses on lifting the energy of the team, and team members take actions according to their shakti levels. A culture that fights for three important projects, rather than swimming in an overwhelming amount of minutiae. And a culture of integrity, where team members can count on each other to do what they say.

Three things to do

1 Pick three projects within your team that you are going to focus on and fight for over the next 90 days.

2 Introduce the idea of failing 50 per cent to your team. Invite everyone in your team to set some stretch goals for the next 90 days that they intend to fail half of. The paradox here is that we are completely committed to each individual project and we give everything to succeed, but when we step back and look at the whole portfolio of projects, it is our expectation, and even our intent, that half will fail.

3 Ask each of the team members how committed they are, as a number out of 10, to the projects that you are focusing on.

Chapter 10

———— PROJECTS ————

Far better it is to dare mighty things, to win glorious triumphs, even though checkered by failure, than to take rank with those poor spirits who neither enjoy much nor suffer much, because they live in the gray twilight that knows not victory nor defeat.

Theodore Roosevelt, former US President

We saw in the discussion of the personal domain in part I that everything we do falls into one of five categories: instinct, response, habit, system or project. And we saw that projects are what rock, and that they are also the hardest to do.

When we look at the behaviour of teams, instincts disappear, and as we can see in the team projects model (figure 10.1, overleaf), the line now passes between systems and projects. To the left of the line is business as usual. The area to the left is where the core business of a team or organisation happens, and the more efficient this is the better. To the right of the line is where new stuff is created, and where the biggest payoffs live. The projects that matter are what makes a team inspiring for its members. The elements to the left of the line pay the bills.

Figure 10.1: team projects model

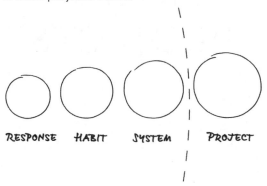

Response

Within your team there are responses to stimuli that are either internal (from the team) or external (from customers, suppliers or other stakeholders). Let's imagine that Jane is a surgeon, and she has a team that performs surgery with her. The types of things that the surgery team might respond to are:

- the phone ringing with information that an ambulance is on the way to the hospital
- an email arriving calling a team meeting
- a patient starting to bleed internally during surgery.

Generally the easiest type of work is to respond to something — we don't have to overcome the inertia of working out what to do, we simply respond to an external stimuli. Response is also why it's easy to lose a lot of time to emails. It doesn't take much to respond to an email that has come in. The risk is that we don't think about whether responding is important or a high priority and so answering an email can take the place of more important activities.

Some jobs are almost 100 per cent responding. You arrive at work, respond to emails, phone calls, meetings—that are all part of someone else's projects.

There are exceptions to this—responding is not always easy. If you're part of a terrorist response team, for example, a response to a terrorist act would be much more challenging than it is for you or I to respond to an email. But for the most part, responding to a stimulus takes less energy than the other elements on the team projects model.

Habit

Things also happen habitually. The Monday morning team meeting, for example. Habits are great because they reduce the amount of energy required to get things done.

If we come back to Jane's surgical team, some of their habits might be the following:

- Lee always stands to Jane's left, Dinh to her right.

- The team does a quick check-in at the start of a procedure, gives a brief report of how they are feeling, and mentally prepares for the surgery they are about to perform.

- The instruments are laid out the same way every day.

Some of our habits serve the team, and some don't. It is worth identifying which habits we want to develop, which we want to keep, and which we want to get rid of. Within our teams we want to develop the habits that will make it easier for us to implement the projects that matter.

TEAM

Systems

Teams also usually have systems in place that they are obliged to follow, known as procedures. Jane's team might have the following systems:

- a standard system for processing new patients
- a systematic way for performing a given surgery
- a checklist to follow when they are completing an operation.

The industrial revolution was built around having workers respond to stimuli, build habits and follow systems—and nothing else. The factory is an efficiency-driven system; it was not designed to foster new projects or innovation.

Paradoxically, great systems are the key to allowing great projects to happen. If our systems aren't good, all our energy goes into our core business. If we don't have systems in place for managing the things that happen, extra thinking, work and energy goes into our behaviour for dealing with them every time they have to be done. That is energy that is no longer available for projects—the things that really matter.

Projects

Finally, moving to the right of the line in the team projects model in figure 10.1 (see p. 118) there are the projects that we launch as a team.

For example, using Jane's team again, they might launch the following projects:

- learning how to perform a new procedure they don't currently do

- writing a white paper about their particular field of expertise

- increasing the effectiveness of post-operative rehabilitation by 50 per cent

- enrolling the rest of the hospital to adopt a methodology they have been using effectively.

You can see there is a different flavour to the projects we launch from those of everything else we do. Projects are more challenging, more demanding and take more of us than anything to the left of the line.

While there can be high levels of satisfaction doing a good job using responses, habits and systems, the juice is definitely in the projects. This is where the risk, joy, fulfilment and breakthrough results are to be found.

A 21st century résumé is increasingly a description of projects that were implemented. A good test for how well you, as a manager, are empowering your team to implement projects that matter is to ask yourself the following: *'Which projects would my team members be proud enough of to put on their résumés?'*

TEAM

IN SUMMARY

To free up the time, energy and resources to implement the projects that matter, everything else needs to happen smoothly. Make sure the best of you and your team goes into your projects: the high-energy times, the best thinking and the highest attention.

While systems are managed and tasks are managed, you simply can't 'manage' the creation of great projects in the same way. Many management roles exist to manage those things that are left of the line. The manager responds to instructions and makes decisions, but doesn't create projects. These managers, and their teams, hardly ever do important work on their own.

It's critical to recognise where a given piece of work lives in the project model—is it a response, a habit, a system or a project—and then treat it accordingly.

Great teams are project-driven. If you want to have an engaged, switched-on, productive team doing their best work, projects are essential.

Three things to do

1 Track how much time in your team is spent on responses, habits, systems and projects.

2 Invite everyone on the team to pick three projects that they are fighting for in their personal lives. Download the white paper at www.newrulesofmanagement.com for everyone on the team, or give them this book to read.

3 Document the three projects that your team is currently focused on, using the Project on a Page template that you can download at www.newrulesofmanagement.com.

Chapter 11

—— FRAMEWORK ——

Seek, above all, for a game worth playing.
Such is the advice of the oracle to the modern man.
Having found the game, play it with intensity — play as
if your life and sanity depended on it ... Follow the
example of the French existentialists and flourish a
banner bearing the word 'engagement'.

Robert S. de Ropp, author of *The Master Game*

Within our teams, the projects we create and execute sit within an overall framework, a model of which is shown in figure 11.1 (overleaf). The framework answers the questions why we implement, how we do it, and where. It's made up of our context, our method and our environment. Within the team domain the focus for our framework is that it is shared. It is critical that the team is aligned on the why, the where and the how of major projects.

As we saw in chapter 5, all projects are implemented within an overall framework that gives the context, the environment and the method for the creation and execution of the endeavour. The implementation framework model contains all these elements, and this chapter looks at how to set up an effective framework within a team that is implementing projects that matter.

Figure 11.1: implementation framework model

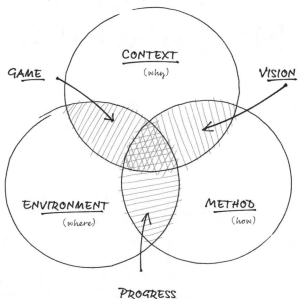

Context: why

Our context is, at the highest level, *why* we implement projects. It includes the purpose that the team has come together for, and the overall vision for the project.

Five weeks before our child Scarlett was due to be born, we finally got planning permission for the two-bedroom home we wanted to build on my parents' property. So the question for us was should we have a crack at getting the house built before Scarlett arrived, or should we wait.

Life was going to be much easier with a baby in the new house, but on the other hand, who ever heard of a house being built in five weeks? (And, incidentally, I had to write this book in the same five weeks).

I called Gerry, my builder, and we went through the plans. He thought it could be done. Nobody else did. Everyone thought we were crazy to try it, and that it would be a nightmare: Scarlett would arrive, and we'd be in the spare room at my parents' place. Not the ideal scenario.

So we decided to go for it. We figured that while it wouldn't be great if Scarlett came along when we were halfway through, there also wasn't going to be a convenient time any time soon, and that Gerry was free and could put a crew together straight away, so we got started.

The challenge wasn't so much the timeline, but the sequencing of all the trades. The tiler couldn't start before the plaster was done, but we couldn't get the plasterer in before the plumber and electrician had roughed in their bits, which could only happen when the building was at a certain point, and so on. It would take only one tradie to let us down for the whole thing to go pear-shaped, as viewers of *Grand Design* would know.

So for five weeks we kept talking to Scarlett in Trish's tummy, telling her she couldn't come out until the book was finished and the house was built. Gerry and the crew worked like crazy and our motto was 'whatever it takes' (with apologies to Prakash Menon for stealing his mantra).

And after five weeks and one day (we were a day late) we moved in. Luckily Scarlett was 10 days late, so we were all good.

The thing that made the difference was that everyone involved bought into the context for the project. Everyone was on board to get the house built before Scarlett arrived — and Trish waddling around the building site nine months pregnant was a good reminder of the deadline. When the plasterer was due to start on Monday, we had the electrician in on Saturday, and the

TEAM

plumber in on Sunday so the plasterer could start on time. The guys all worked evenings and weekends when needed. For the whole team it was a project worth doing. The context was not just another house, or business as usual: it was get the house done before Trish had her baby.

And funnily enough, since Scarlett was born our plumber has reverted to type (with apologies to all the plumbers out there). He had done everything that was needed for us to move in, but the external stuff was still incomplete. Open trenches, downpipes not connected to storm water, and so on. The initial build took five weeks. The last 10 per cent? Three months.

The Watson project at IBM gives us another great example of a project with a powerful context, and the difference that makes. It all began in 2007 when an IBM executive came up with an unusual idea over dinner. His exact words, quoted on the IBM website: 'If you could get a computer to play *Jeopardy*, gee that'd capture people's imaginations.'

Jeopardy is America's most popular quiz show. A computer winning Jeopardy is much harder than it seems at first, because it would require new levels of natural language recognition, processing speeds and more. For example having a computer answer a question like 'Which American city has its largest airport named for a World War II hero and its second largest for a World War II battle?' is very different from asking it 'What's 7 x 9?'.

A major project, called IBM Watson, was developed from this simple idea. Projects of this nature are developed in the IBM Thomas J. Watson Research Centre, the headquarters for research at IBM—the largest industrial research organisation in the world, with eight labs in six countries.

In 2007 IBM asked its computer scientist and researcher Dave Ferrucci to lead the team to create IBM Watson, a supercomputer that could win on *Jeopardy*. He took a collaborative approach to building the supercomputer, and ended up teaching his team to act like a start-up company within IBM.

The project took four years and, on average, about 20 to 25 people per year in the core team. Other parts of IBM also helped to develop what was needed to finally deliver Watson to play *Jeopardy*, and of course, IBM brought other hardware resources to bear. The project offered an extraordinary opportunity for staff to work on a project of great magnitude and complexity. That meant IBM had to adapt its culture to make it work. Typically, people in research are working on ideas quite slowly — at the pace of traditional scientific research. However, this project had to move much faster. When the team was put together, the focus was on performance and a rapid innovation cycle, and a fairly sizable investment had to be made in hardware infrastructure.

In early 2011, Watson, the computer that had been four years in the making, made its big debut in front of a US national audience on *Jeopardy*. On the left and right stood Brad Ritter and Ken Jennings, the two greatest *Jeopardy* champions in history. In the middle was the computer screen representing Watson. It made for an unusual sight. Watson was connected to a buzzer just like Brad and Ken, heard the questions at the same time, and answered in English.

At the end of the show Watson was the clear winner, with a score triple that of the two human contestants. You can see a 10-minute video of the show on the IBM website, and a longer TED talk about the implications of this called *Final Jeopardy! And the future of Watson* (if you put that into an internet search engine you will find it).

Like the first time a computer beat a chess grand-master in a game of chess, this was a historic moment. The team was clearly moved. The vision of the project from the start was crystal clear: build a computer that can win *Jeopardy*. After the

TEAM

show, Dave Ferrucci spoke of the bigger context of 'research into deep analytics and natural language understanding and taking that technology to solve problems that people really care about. We're so excited about all we can do with this.'

For any project you are asking your team to commit to, give them a purpose worth fighting for. A context powerful enough that they too will be excited to be part of it, and want to do their best work.

Environment: where

The success of our teams, and the individual fulfilment of our team members, comes down to creating and executing projects that matter. Yet more often than not the environments that we show up to work in are not set up to help that happen.

Harvard University recently opened its first lab for innovation and entrepreneurship, with the goal of spurring innovative ventures across the university. In the innovation labs, student teams have shared space to work on their ventures, access to experienced entrepreneurs-in-residence, support from faculty and administrators, and a program of related activities to deepen their understanding of entrepreneurship and innovation.

In other words, it is an environment specifically created to support the implementation of projects that matter.

I think this is really smart. We mostly undervalue the impact our environment has on us. None of us would ever say that a project failed because we didn't have enough plants in the office, or the environment didn't support us. And yet we all feel very different in different environments. Imagine an exquisite Japanese restaurant—you walk through a perfect rock garden, around a tranquil pond with fish swimming, and over a bridge to a hardwood deck. As you cross the deck, the bamboo doors swing open, and you can hear faint music coming from within.

The incense strikes you next, as you are escorted to a private dining room. Compare that scenario to walking off a busy street, into a fast food restaurant, kids screaming, and so on. The environment makes a difference.

Think about the environment you are creating for your team to implement the projects that matter. Be conscious of the light, the images, the sounds, the level of order versus clutter, the configuration of the space, what's on the walls, and so on. Is it a Japanese garden or a fast food restaurant? What you could do to improve the environment and make it more supportive of implementing important projects?

Method: how

A critical success factor for any project is methodology — knowing how to go about executing the project.

Have you ever wondered why, during the Korean War, the American F-86 Sabre managed to score a 10:1 victory ratio over the Russian MiG-15 that the Koreans flew, despite the fact that by most measures the Russian fighter was a superior plane — it could fly higher and further, turn tighter, and climb and accelerate faster? Of course you have!

Well, in any case, John Boyd wondered about that very thing. A fighter pilot during the Korean conflict, and military strategist and fighter instructor, Boyd observed that the F-86's fully hydraulic controls, which allowed a pilot to transition more quickly from one manoeuvre to another, also allowed him to neutralise and overcome what should have been the MiG's technical superiority.

Boyd concluded that all combat involves a cycle of observation, orientation, decision and action — which he named OODA loops. Under OODA loop theory, every combatant observes the situation, orients himself, decides what to do and does it.

If his opponent can do this faster, however, his own actions become outdated and disconnected to the true situation, and his opponent's advantage increases geometrically.

Silicon Valley entrepreneur Eric Ries describes a similar approach in *The Lean Startup*. A core component of his Lean Startup methodology is the build-measure-learn feedback loop. He recommends first determining the problem that needs to be solved and then developing a minimum viable product (MVP) to solve that problem and begin the process of learning as quickly as possible. Once the MVP is established, the product can be improved by iterations of the build-measure-learn loop.

Within teams, successful project implementation incorporates feedback loops. While Boyd calls these OODA loops — observation, orientation, decision and action, Ries talks about feedback loops as build, measure, learn. You would rarely launch a new product or offering without getting some feedback from your market along the way.

Effective teams make these feedback loops as fast as possible. On a macro scale this means implementing more projects, and failing them fast and cheap. On an individual project level, fast feedback loops mean building a prototype, or MVP, as quickly as possible, and then adjusting, or pivoting. If your team can get 10 of these loops completed in the time it takes your competition to do three, you win (even if your competition is smarter and better resourced).

Game

At the intersection of context and environment is game (see figure 11.1, p. 124). Within our teams, the more the project feels like a game, and the more it has the energy of play, the more likely it is to succeed. Jason Fox, the motivation design expert we met in chapter 5, says:

One of the things that enhances performance within team-based games, like any sport or cooperative video games, is visibility. All good games will have a clear goal or purpose — and measures to track performance against these. When you join any good team game, you enter into a shared agreement over the goals you are working to achieve and the rules you'll play by (budget, time frame, boundaries, roles etc).

Some project teams embrace this approach through rituals like daily stand up meetings, where everyone shares their actions and their wins. In this game, you can see what everyone is doing, and how that is impacting upon progress towards the goal. Likewise, they can see you too. There's complete visibility and clarity. And, in an open ecology like this, it's very hard to get away with apathy — which is a great thing!

The news website www.informationweek.com give us a great example of game design in action with Blue Shield, a major US health plan. Blue Shield has jumped on the social gaming and networking trend in fitness and wellness applications. Blue Shield of California is already offering two programs to its employees to drive its employee wellness program. It launched an application called Shape Up Shield that focuses on increasing physical activity:

> This is an eight-week-long, social-media-fueled challenge that uses an online platform to let employees form teams, post comments in forums, set team and personal fitness goals, and give virtual 'high fives' for encouragement. In 2011, over 1,800 Shape Up Shield participants walked, hiked and ran 600 million steps, about 300,000 miles.

One of Blue Shield's new programs, the Daily Challenge from MeYou Health, is similar to Shape Up Shield, in that it uses social media, including Facebook, to make wellness fun. Instead of confining itself to physical exercise, this program gives participants a series of individually tailored Daily Challenges.

The Daily Challenge is a simple activity designed to improve wellbeing. That might be physical, emotional, or mental. The MeYou website says: 'the Daily Challenge promotes everyday wellbeing by encouraging the small actions and fostering the social ties that drive meaningful change. MeYou's program features the hallmarks of social gaming, such as points, badges, status, and progression.'

Eighty per cent of Blue Shield employees have participated in at least one of these two wellness programs featuring game design and social media components. During that period, there has been a 50 per cent drop in smoking, and a 50 per cent increase in regular physical activity among employees. The incidence of hypertension has fallen by two-thirds, and disability claims have also fallen among participating workers, but not among other employees. Pretty remarkable results from introducing a couple of games.

Wherever possible, bring the energy of a game to your team's projects. Make it fun to be part of, have a clear scoreboard, clear rules and an experience of progress. All good game design includes progress, so let's explore that in a bit more detail.

Progress

At the intersection of context and method on the implementation framework model (see figure 11.1, p. 124) lies progress.

Teresa Amabile, author of *The Progress Principle: Using Small Wins to Ignite Joy, Engagement, and Creativity at Work*, is the Edsel Bryant Ford Professor of Business Administration and a director of research at Harvard Business School. Amabile's research encompasses creativity, productivity, innovation and inner work life. She looks at how work methodology, management styles and motivation affect productivity. Her findings were published in her book, and in the *Harvard Business Review* in January 2010.

Amabile surveyed more than 600 managers from dozens of companies to rank the impact on employee motivation and emotions of five workplace factors commonly considered significant: recognition, incentives, interpersonal support, progress and clear goals.

Have a look at those five motivators. How would you rank them? Which of them do you use to motivate your team? If you are like the majority of managers, you would rank recognition number one. Unfortunately, those managers are wrong.

We know this because Amabile also completed a multiyear study tracking the day-to-day activities, emotions, and motivation levels of hundreds of knowledge workers in a wide variety of settings. The top motivator of performance is progress. Amazingly, it's the factor those managers surveyed ranked dead last.

On days when workers have the sense they're making headway in their jobs, or when they receive support that helps them overcome obstacles and make progress, their emotions are most positive and their drive to succeed is at its peak. On days when they feel they are spinning their wheels or encountering roadblocks to meaningful accomplishment, and not making progress, their moods and motivation are lowest.

It turns out that an experience of progress is more important than clear goals, recognition, incentives or anything else when it comes to team members feeling positive about a project, and doing their best work. So it makes sense to incorporate lots of milestones in the framework of the project, and focus on ensuring team members experience a sense of progress. As we saw earlier, an experience of progress towards a goal is one of the elements Jason Fox talks about as critical to good game design.

TEAM

Vision

Vision sits at the intersection of context and method, as you saw in figure 11.1 (see p. 124).

The job of the team leader is to inspire and unite the team. While progress is a great motivator (and as the research described earlier indicates, it may be the best motivator), there needs to be progress towards something. And that something is the vision: a clear picture of what the team is setting out to achieve. Ideally something that is inspiring, and something that the team can unite around.

One of the most famous US football pre-game speeches of all time was all about painting a vision. In 2005 the Super Bowl was played between the New England Patriots and the Philadelphia Eagles. For Australian readers, the Super Bowl is like the AFL grand final, only much more so — much bigger, and of course much more American. It's the biggest annual sporting event in the world.

At the heart of New England Patriots' coach Bill Belichick's pre-game speech was his undying devotion to Rudyard Kipling's philosophy that, 'the strength of the Wolf is the Pack'. Belichick subscribes so passionately to his belief in the team that it has left an imprint on the National Football League in the United States.

Belichick's pre-game speech that year hammered home his doctrine. He pointed to the Lombardi trophy that the winners receive and asked, 'What's that symbolise? Not the guy who leads the league in punting. Not the guy who's got 15 sacks. Not the guy who's got 1200 yards rushing [all individual milestones]. It represents the team. That's the toughest, smartest, most competent team.' When he pointed to the trophy, he was imprinting on his players the vision of winning the game, and he went on to describe the picture of how they would win. As a team, not as individuals. Needless to say, they won the game, the Super Bowl and the trophy.

One of your most important jobs as a manager of a team is to paint the vision of victory. What does successfully implementing the project look like? Tell the story of the future where the project has been completed as vividly as possible.

For any important project, it's worth imagining that rather than being paid, the team on the project are all volunteers. What would you need to do to attract people to the project if it wasn't their job, and they didn't have to do it in order to get paid?

What's the vision for the project that would be inspiring enough to attract a team? What's the context, or purpose, they could all get behind? What environment would you need to create that they would want to show up and come to work in? What's the methodology that would keep them going? How would you incorporate game design and the experience of progress into the project?

TEAM

——————— IN SUMMARY ———————

As we can see from the implementation framework model (see p. 124), there are six critical elements to creating a powerful framework for your team to implement within. We want a context that pulls us forward, so describe a purpose that is worth getting out of bed for. Create an environment for your team that makes it a pleasure to come to work (both the physical environment and the digital one). Have a clear implementation methodology for implementing projects. Play some games, and bring the energy of games into the work and the projects. Include milestones, and give everyone the experience of progress, given that's the greatest motivator. And finally, paint a vision that the team would run through brick walls to get to.

Three things to do

1   Clarify the purpose and vision of the team projects with the team. Make sure that everyone is aligned to it and that it is inspiring.

2   Create displays of the progress of the major projects within the environment.

3   Inject some game design into your three key projects, and ensure team members will experience progress along the way.

Chapter 12

SUPPORT

*The best executive is the one who has sense enough to pick
good men to do what he wants done, and self-restraint to
keep from meddling with them while they do it.*

Theodore Roosevelt, former US president.

One of the biggest differences between implementing individual
projects and implementing team projects is the interaction
between different personalities within the team. Some teams
have a great balance of personalities and skills, but nearly all
teams will need the assistance and support of people outside
the team at some point. Understanding the strengths and
weaknesses of your team, and where you can get external
support from, will improve your chances of success. As you can
see in the team support model shown in figure 12.1 (overleaf),
the four key support roles for a team are: advisers, buddies,
assistants and champions.

Let's look at an inspiring team that came together for a significant
project, and then examine how these four roles worked.

Figure 12.1: team support model

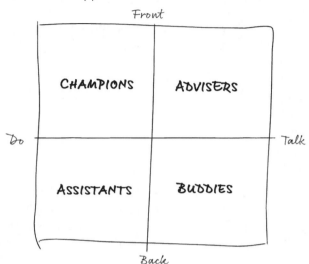

On Saturday 7 February 2009 the state of Victoria suffered its worst natural disaster, a bushfire that became known as Black Saturday. The temperature was 46°C, and there were very high winds, reaching in excess of 100 kilometres per hour. The state had experienced an intense heat wave and almost two months of little or no rain on top of a decade of drought. There were more than 400 fire incidents that day; 173 people died and more than 2000 houses were destroyed by the fires.

Flowerdale—a small country town about 100 kilometres north-east of Melbourne—lost 235 houses, and 13 people died. No emergency services entered the town until four days after the fires.

Pete Williams, one of the key members of the Flowerdale community team, told me the story of how the team came together after the fires. He believes that it was because there was no external support from emergency services in the early days that the team formed so powerfully.

The community organised its own recovery. They said, 'We've got a problem and we're going to solve it ourselves'. The first community meeting was held at 9.00 am the day after the fire—and that was when the team formed. There was a community meeting every day for the next eight weeks.

As momentum built within the community it became very apparent that what Pete Williams calls 'the "Do-Ocracy" style' of getting things moving—by the community team— was orders of magnitude better than the response from the government in other fire-stricken towns.

The community team was also effective at bringing in advisers. One was Bob Dixson, the mayor of Greensburgh in Kansas, USA, which had been destroyed by a tornado in May 2007 and recovered effectively. He visited Flowerdale after the fire and gave guidance on the structure of the community team and their meetings. General Peter Cosgrove, former head of the defence forces in Australia and a veteran of reorganisation in East Timor and after Cyclone Larry, also contributed in an advisory capacity.

Philanthropists also came to the immediate relief of the town. Andrew 'Twiggy' Forrest, one of Australia's richest people, flew in on his helicopter a week after the fires and was the first person who really asked what was needed. The community said they wanted to create a temporary village to avoid population flight and potential collapse of the town—something that was viewed as an impossible goal and something that had never been done before in Australia. Forrest provided more than a dozen miners' huts that got the village moving.

However, the main support came from Sheikh Mohammed of Dubai through his racing and breeding arm, Darley, which contacted the community team and told them it had a big budget and wanted to deal directly with communities. This gave the team the opportunity to create a vision for the town, rather than just react as they had been. So they created a vision of a sustainable town, which was presented, and was the basis of the donation from the sheikh. The relationship continues to this day.

Three years later the town is largely rebuilt, and the community's vision of a sustainable town is being realised. Every public building is now solar powered. A lot of the facilities the town had wanted for many years are now in place, from a men's shed to a purpose-built kindergarten attached to the school. The school is only small but enrolments are now at 43, against 33 at the time the fires hit, which is a great sign for any small country town that could well have disappeared altogether after being virtually burnt to the ground.

Advisers

Advisers are talkers who have your front. They will ask the questions that enable you to come to your own decisions. They will encourage you to think things through rather than rush into a decision.

In the Flowerdale project, the team obviously had no experience in disaster relief, or of what was involved in rebuilding a town and a community. One of the keys to the success of the project was the calibre of the advisers they managed to bring in. There were many more, but the two I mentioned were Bob Dixson, the mayor of Greensburgh, and General Peter Cosgrove.

Both had relevant experience and were able to provide invaluable guidance. The CSIRO (Australia's national science agency — the Commonwealth Scientific and Industrial Research Organisation) also provided experts in water management, integrated planning and bushfire safety, who ran workshops in an advisory capacity for the town.

Buddies

It is extremely useful to have buddies you can talk to at a peer level when the going gets tough. Often this is an informal arrangement, and a buddy is definitely not someone you report to.

In the Flowerdale project, talking to buddies, or peers, was achieved through the daily community meetings. While the project team had a more formal weekly status meeting, at the daily community meeting people could check in, share what was going on for them and support each other.

Assistants

Assistants are the doers who have your back: they are the people you can count on for decisiveness and reliability, and they will get things done for you without complication. They are the people who do all the background tasks that free up the rest of the team to progress the project itself.

In the Flowerdale example, the government agencies eventually provided the assistance that the team needed to get the job done. But when the government tried to take over the project, everything ground to a halt—it just didn't have the same motivation and flexibility to do what was needed. It was only when government took the role of assisting the community team to implement the project of reconstruction that everything worked.

Lots of other assistance came from various trade unions for building the temporary village, and from many other volunteers.

Typically the role of assistants, in this case the volunteers, is to perform the background tasks and allow the other team members to focus on the more strategic tasks. In many projects, providing some administrative or background support can free up the team to focus on the critical tasks that will make the project successful.

TEAM

Champions

Champions are the people who go into bat for the teams and the projects they believe in. It is often useful to have people outside the team who are champions for the project and the team.

The obvious champions for the Flowerdale project were the philanthropists—in particular Andrew 'Twiggy' Forrest and Sheikh Mohammed of Dubai, although there were many, many more. They all gave resources, and publicly championed the project.

Champions don't necessarily provide financial support, but they publicly back the project in some way.

IN SUMMARY

As a manager, one of the most important things you can do for your team to ensure their projects have the best chance of success is to provide the support they need. The team support model shown in figure 12.1 (see p. 138) divides the supporters into those out front, and those that have our back, as well as those that we talk to and those that do the doing. There are advisers who are in front and talk; buddies who are at the back and talk; assistants who have your back and do the doing; and finally champions, who are out front and also do the doing.

Three things to do

1   For each of your key projects identify all the support people you have, and categorise them into advisers, buddies, assistants or champions.

2   Where there are gaps in the support roles, determine if those roles should be filled, and who would be the ideal people to fill those roles.

3   Invite those people onto the project team.

Chapter 13
– ACCOUNTABILITY –

The quality of a leader is reflected in the standards they set for themselves.

Ray Kroc, Entrepreneur behind McDonalds brand

In ancient times, the Greek leader Xenophon and his mercenaries were being pursued by a huge army of Persians. He decided the time had come to turn and fight. He chose the spot, but one of his officers reputedly said: 'I don't think this is a good spot to make our stand. There is a cliff behind us: there is no way for us to retreat if things are going badly.'

Xenophon's reply was something like: 'Exactly! In fact, we are going to march our army until our backs are up to the cliff, and that way the Persians will also know there is no way we can retreat. We are going to fight to the death.'

A slightly less brutal example comes out of Ireland. I remember travelling through the Emerald Isle, and being struck not only by how green everything was, but also by the way that fences were built from stones rather than posts and wire like we have in Australia. Local legend has it that it would not be uncommon to come across a wall high enough to seem insurmountable.

The practice in this situation was to throw your hat over the wall. That way, even if you couldn't see over and couldn't see a way to scale it, if your hat was on the other side, you had no choice but to work it out.

Nobel Prize–winning economist Thomas Shelling writes about this approach to commitment in terms of what he calls 'arranging things so that you can't compromise'. I love that idea—arranging the circumstances so that you can't compromise. That's what a good accountability structure does. It puts your back to the cliff, burns your boats and arranges your world so that you can't compromise.

A good accountability structure is a critical component of implementing projects that matter. As we know, projects are difficult, and generally there is a point when we will need to push through. The right level of accountability helps our teams do this.

As the accountability level rises, so do the stakes. Where the accountability is personal—only to ourselves—we will be disappointed if we pull out, but the disappointment is only with ourselves. Often that's not enough to encourage us to persevere with a project—when that's the case, we need a higher level of accountability. We need to move further along the accountability model (see figure 13.1).

Private

Sometimes, within our teams and organisations, private accountability is sufficient.

At IBM, a successful private accountability strategy is used through its social media presence. There is no organisational mandate for social media: it is up to each individual if they participate, and to what degree.

Figure 13.1: the accountability model

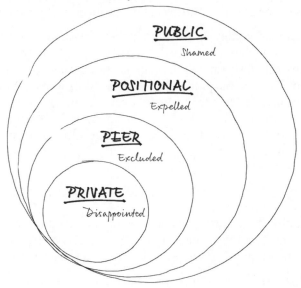

According to news website socialtimes.com, IBM doesn't have a corporate blog or a corporate Twitter ID because the company wants all 'IBMers' to be the corporate blog and the corporate Twitter ID, collectively. IBM lets employees talk—to each other and to the public—without intervention. Socialtimes. com also recorded some IBM social media facts and stats:

- no IBM corporate blog or Twitter account

- 17 000 internal blogs

- 10 000 employees using internal blogs (from a total of 400 000 employees around the world)

- thousands of external bloggers

- almost 200 000 on LinkedIn.

In this vibrant forum, employees exchange ideas, advance conversations and do a little self-promotion of their projects.

All of this is achieved through private accountability. Each employee chooses their level of participation in the various social media platforms, and is accountable only to themselves for their level of participation. If an IBM employee wants to start a blog, and decides to write every week, no-one is going to check up on them. It's not part of their job description, and they don't get paid to do it. They are only accountable to themselves to keep going.

Peer

Accountability to one's teammates is much more powerful than accountability to oneself. Where there is a strong culture within a team, members don't want to let their teammates down.

Australian software company Atlassian uses what it calls FedEx Days every few months, when the employees go into a conference and start discussing ideas for dramatically improving their key products, JIRA or Confluence. The goal is to put a range of ideas out on the table and then spend the rest of the day working to turn the most promising notions into bits of code. There's more about FedEx Days in chapter 16.

With all of their regular tasks put on hold for the day, the developers are free to imagine, argue, and code. As reported on Atlassian's website (www.atlassian.com), there are only two stipulations:

- First, their efforts have to be 'out of the ordinary'; they cannot work on something that was already in the product development roadmap.

- Second, by the day's end they have to deliver a working prototype.

The day concludes with a show-and-tell over pizza and beer—true peer accountability that is made fun.

Atlassian's software is highly modular, which makes it easy for engineers to develop extensions, known as plug-ins, that enhance the core product. Atlassian holds two to three FedEx Days a year, and reports that some of its most productive and innovative work comes from these days.

No bonuses or overtime are paid for these 24 hours, and yet people will work through the night. Teams form spontaneously to work on a project for the 24 hours, and will do anything not to let each other down, and to complete something extraordinary. It's a great example of the power of peer accountability.

Positional

Positional accountability to the team leader, or to the boss, where the implementation of the project is part of a job description and tied into performance reviews and potentially to remuneration, is more powerful again than personal or peer accountability.

Accenture, the consulting firm I worked for out of university, uses predominantly positional accountability to fulfil on big, expensive, long-term projects. An Accenture project that I was involved with was the installation and customisation of an enterprise-wide software system called SAP.

Typically each different part of the business had different software packages—so the warehouse might have one type of software, the manufacturing plant another, customer service a third, finance a fourth, and so on. Generally these different software packages didn't do a good job of speaking to each other, and as you can imagine—and have probably experienced—this caused problems. For example, if you changed your address and let the customer service people know, they would update their database. But the finance department wouldn't necessarily find out and so they would still send your bill to the old address—maybe not such a bad thing. But then the warehouse might not get the memo either, and they would ship your stuff to your old house, and that's no fun for anyone.

In the mid 1990s a new class of software emerged to address this problem. It was called Enterprise Resource Planning software, or ERP, and the idea was that one piece of software could manage the whole company—so an update somewhere would be seen by everyone. Done properly, this increases efficiency, improves the customer experience and makes life easier for the staff.

SAP was the biggest of these ERP systems, and that's what we were installing for the client. We had a team of about 50 people from Accenture working on the project, and that many again from the client company. The software itself cost millions of dollars, and the bill from Accenture to the client would have been tens of millions—although I was too far down the food chain to be involved in those discussions.

The project ran for a year and was executed almost entirely using positional accountability. There was a clear hierarchy in the project. Within Accenture, analysts reported to consultants, consultants reported to managers, and the managers reported to partners. I was an analyst and my consultant would give me a piece of code to write. He told me what to do, how to do it, and when it had to be done by. I never got to see the whole picture of the project, just the cog I was working on.

For projects of that magnitude, positional accountability works well. It did in that project, and it is probably the right level of accountability for a project of that magnitude and complexity.

Public

The most powerful level of accountability is *public*. This occurs when everyone within the team knows that the whole world, or at least a significant part of it, will know whether the project is a success or a failure.

As part of London's 2005 bid for the 2012 Summer Olympic and Paralympic Games, bid chairman, British politician and former athlete Sebastian Coe made a pledge to harness the events to inspire two million individuals to take up sport and physical activity. In 2007 the UK government published its Olympic legacy plans in the Department for Culture, Media and Sport's Legacy Promises document. Its five promises were to:

- make the UK a world-leading sporting nation

- transform the heart of East London

- inspire a generation of young people to take part in local volunteering, and in cultural and physical activity

- make the Olympic Park a blueprint for sustainable living

- demonstrate that the UK is a creative, inclusive and welcoming place to live in, visit and conduct business.

This was a substantial commitment to broaden the benefits of hosting the games beyond the usual predictions of economic gain. And London could be sure that the world would be watching carefully, given the apparent failure of many host cities to realise promised benefits, often even being saddled with debt for decades after.

The pledge was especially potent for Londoners. The five boroughs around Stratford that would be involved with

TEAM

the Olympic facilities had been shown to have problems in many areas when compared with London averages. These included high levels of obesity, low levels of physical activity, high levels of smoking, poor educational levels, low levels of employment or training for teenagers, and a high number of court appearances for young people.

The British government formed the Olympic Park Legacy Company and the London Legacy Corporation to implement these commitments. Between them, it was proposed that they would manage the assets and responsibilities of a number of regeneration agencies, including the Queen Elizabeth Olympic Park (the name of the Olympic Park after the Games finished), to promote and deliver the promised physical, social, economic and environmental regeneration in the Olympic Park and surrounding area.

In 2009, the London boroughs that would host the 2012 Games also published their plans for how they would ensure a legacy from the Games. Their stated goal was that, by 2030, the host communities would have the same or greater social and economic life chances as the London average.

London's publication of its pledges and plans have turned the world's attention to their the Olympic Legacy project, creating public accountability for the team charged with seeing it through. Failing is not an option: failure would not only be visible to itself, but also visible to countless spectators around the globe.

From the point at which you create public accountability for your team, there is no other way to go but to move forward and fulfil the crowd's expectations—which are your team's own goals that you have simply broadcast to more people. Ultimately, this means that you have more people pushing the team to succeed.

─────── IN SUMMARY ───────

Projects that matter are not easy for teams to implement. The appropriate accountability structure makes it much more likely that the team will succeed in implementing its projects. We saw earlier that integrity—doing what you say—is a key part of creating an implementation culture within a team. The right accountability structure supports doing what you say, and helps team members stay true to their commitments.

Three things to do

1   Determine the appropriate accountability level for each project that the team is focused on.

2   Discuss the accountability levels with the team, and implement these accountability structures.

3   Invite team members to share their personal projects to create peer accountability within the team for their personal projects.

PART III

—ORGANISATION—

Chapter 14
ORGANISATION
—————— OVERVIEW ——————

*If you are the smartest person in the room,
you are in the wrong room.*

Friedrich Nietzsche, philosopher

The old rules of management, the ones taught in MBAs, were created for a different time. And while the 20th century was not that long ago, everything has changed since then — but management practices haven't caught up.

Traditional management practices are all about optimising the existing business and looking after the existing clients. Under the old rules, we would break our market into segments, look at our competitors in each segment and do our competitor analysis, and then fight to increase our market share in these segments. Our profit and share price provided the scoreboard and told us how well we were managing the organisation.

But the world has changed. Everything is faster; product cycles are shorter; and we are swamped with more information than ever before. I remember a few years ago when Google passed a billion searches a month. There are now more than a billion

Google searches a day. That means that on average, every person on the planet searches Google once a week.

Your competitor could now be two kids in a garage, a start-up in Silicon Valley — or in Bangalore, India. Your customers don't know what's best for them, and traditional models of management are failing.

The Innovator's Dilemma by disruptive innovation theorist Clayton Christenson provides stark evidence of this. He demonstrates why outstanding companies that had their competitive antennae up, listened astutely to customers and invested aggressively in new technologies still lost their market dominance, and in many cases went under. Drawing on years of research, and citing examples from many industries (computers, retailing, pharmaceuticals, automobiles, steel), Clayton argues that good companies fail not because of bad management practices, but because of what has traditionally been considered good management. That's huge — good companies are going under because they are doing what they were taught to do, and meeting the needs of their customers.

Christenson shows how truly important, breakthrough innovations — what he calls disruptive innovations — are often initially rejected by customers who cannot currently use them, leading firms to allow their most important innovations to languish. Kodak had the technology for digital cameras ahead of its competitors. In fact, way back in 1975 Kodak developed the world's first digital camera, but at the time its customers didn't want an alternative that was then inferior to film cameras.

So Kodak listened to its customers and stuck with film, putting all its efforts into making that technology better, and competing with other players in that space. What it needed to do was have a small team hived off somewhere competing with the other start-ups playing with digital photography, while the rest of the business kept looking after its existing customers. Unfortunately for Kodak, it came late to the digital party, and while it did achieve a significant market share, it never made money from its digital cameras. Kodak last made a profit in 2007 and filed for bankruptcy in 2012.

Christenson argues that many companies now face the innovator's dilemma—the dilemma Kodak faced between looking after existing customers and innovating for future growth. Keeping close to customers is critical for current success. But long-term growth and profits depend upon a very different managerial formula—what we call the new rules of management, focusing on creating our own disruptive innovations through implementing projects that matter.

A business plan that sets out five-year growth targets with a month-by-month budget is a fantasy in the 21st century. There are way too many assumptions that can never be tested in advance. As a tool for raising funds, a business plan might work. For running a large organisation, it's mostly a waste of time, effort and countless reams of paper.

Indeed, the way that large organisations think about strategy is changing, moving away from a traditional business plan to what I call an implementation plan. An implementation plan says something like: 'We are going to implement 20 great projects in this direction over the next three years. We expect 10 of them to fail. Currently we only know what five of the 20 are. Stay tuned.'

Business and project-management writer Lauren Keller Johnson recognised this trend in her 2008 *Harvard Business Review* article 'Close the gap between projects and strategy'. She recommends that organisations develop a 'project portfolio brain', and think about running the organisation as a portfolio of projects, with portfolio managers, and project-portfolio modelling software.

Global e-business leaders Cathleen Benko and F. Warren McFarlan take this idea even further in their 2003 book *Connecting the Dots: Aligning Projects with Objectives in Unpredictable Times.* They say: 'If you want to find out where your company is going to be three to five years from now, don't look at your stated strategy. Instead, look at your projects'. That's a pretty radical idea—that strategy comes from the rear-vision mirror—rather than guiding everything.

From an implementation perspective, I love it! 'Business as usual' means spending lots of time and energy locked away determining the strategy, and then fitting everything else an organisation does to that strategy. The implementation approach says we're going to launch lots of projects. The ones that succeed—they are our strategy.

The mantra of any great organisation is 'We implement great projects'—and the only way you get to be a great organisation is by implementing great projects. Apple, which in 2012 has the highest market capitalisation of any company in the world (in other words, it's the most valuable publicly listed company on the planet), got there through implementing awesome projects. Not through clever marketing, although it does that pretty well, too, and certainly not through customer service, or more efficient systems, or a better business plan. If you look at the last decade of that organisation it's a story of implementing one great project after another.

If you are not innovating and executing, not implementing, not doing great stuff, you're standing still, and if you're standing still, you're going backwards.

If personal fulfilment comes from doing great work—and we know it does—and organisational success comes from launching great projects, how are we getting this wrong in our organisations? The issue, as we have seen, is that even though we personally get fulfilment from doing great work, we are simply not wired for creating and implementing big projects. Our default position is to be lazy, and we need the workarounds to do the work. Organisations are set up on an industrial revolution model. They focus on managing out the errors; they see people as part of the machine who need to be managed accordingly.

We also measure the wrong things in our organisations. Our primary measures are turnover and profit, and these generally translate into share price. The problem is that these are all lag indicators—profit is generally a measure of the great projects we implemented years ago and are still reaping the rewards from. Implementing a great project now will cost money in the short term, reducing profit and making the numbers look worse. But in the long term these are the projects that will create new markets and new ways to serve existing markets—in short, they provide future growth.

Imagine an oil company that has two primary activities: extracting oil from existing oilfields and exploring to find new fields. The existing fields are the fruits of the previous exploration. To maximise profits this year, the thing to do would be to eliminate all exploration and just pump as much oil as we can from the fields we already have. Of course, this is a short-sighted strategy, but it is pretty much the equivalent of what many organisations do.

You can equate your current core business to the existing oilfields, and the exploration to implementing new projects. While it isn't as obvious, history shows us that selling your existing products to your existing customers is every bit as finite as an oilfield: at some point, sooner or later, it will run dry. Many organisations don't recognise the implementation imperative, and stick to the current core business—the existing oilfields. They do so at their peril.

ORGANISATION

Once again our primary implementation model (see figure 14.1) is the key. In our organisations, as in our teams and our personal lives, projects are created and executed, and require time and energy. The internal component of the model for organisations is climate — the equivalent of culture for a team and mindset for an individual. Let's look at all five elements of the model briefly, and then unpack them for organisations.

Figure 14.1: primary implementation model

Create

PROJECTS | FRAMEWORK

Time — INTERNAL — Energy

ACCOUNTABILITY | SUPPORT

Execute

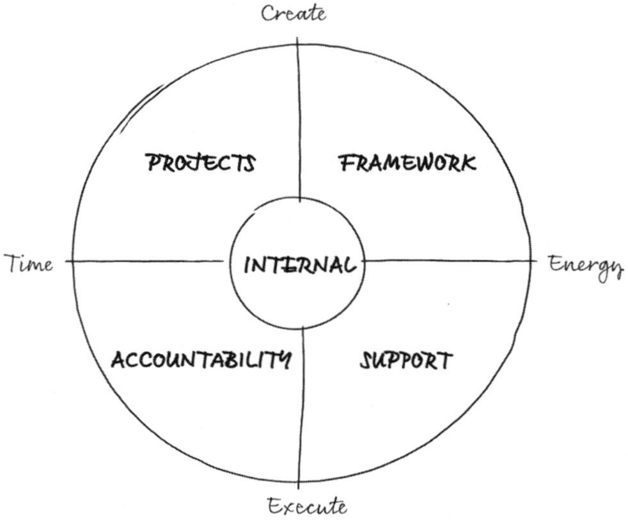

Internal

Many organisations have a climate that discourages the creation and execution of great projects.

These organisations are geared towards maintaining the status quo rather than exploring brave new worlds.

An essential part of implementing great projects at the organisational level is creating an internal climate within the organisation that is conducive to the implementation of great projects. This comes down to the three stages of implementation (*start, persevere and complete*), and *how we are*, *what we do* and *the conversations we have* throughout the whole process. At every stage the organisation's climate can either support the implementation of innovative projects, or hamper it.

Projects

Traditional management is about how to maximise the core business and make incremental improvements to 'business as usual'. When a new, disruptive technology comes along, this approach has unfortunately meant the end of many previously successful, well-managed companies.

For companies to survive disruptive events and grow beyond incremental improvements to an existing business model, they need to create and execute innovative projects that matter. Traditional management practices are inadequate for this task.

Framework

Embarking on projects that matter is a risky endeavour in most organisations, and without the right framework these projects will either never make it to the starting line, or be abandoned at the first sign of difficulty.

The organisation needs to create a context that prioritises implementation; an environment that supports it; and a methodology that enables the creation of projects that matter.

ORGANISATION

Support

Given how challenging it can be to implement the projects that matter, it is critical at an organisational level to have a structure in place to support people, teams and projects. This means helping the people and the teams that are doing the important work by having their front and their back, and assisting them with the doing and the conversations required.

The critical support roles at an organisational level are:

- *expertise* — people to provide know-how that drives results

- *protection* — people who provide an environment for entrepreneurial risk-taking

- *resourcing* — providing the time, money and people to fulfil projects

- *advocacy* — people to champion the projects both internally and externally.

Accountability

Within our organisations there are some things we leave up to the individual's private accountability. Sometimes peer accountability is enough. In organisations, positional accountability, typically reporting to a higher level, is important. And sometimes there is public accountability — accountability to the whole organisation or beyond.

These different levels are like currency that we can spend to focus productivity on the areas that matter, and ensure that the important projects get implemented.

Chapter 15

INTERNAL
——————— CLIMATE ———————

*Avoiding danger is no safer in the long run than outright
exposure. Life is either a daring adventure or nothing.*

Helen Keller, author, political activist, humanitarian

S. T. Hunter, K. E. Bedell and M. D. Mumford, from the University
of Oklahoma, tell us that climate is people's perception and
experience of their work environment. Climate is commonly
explored by asking questions like whether employees feel free
to express their ideas to their boss, or whether people are not
afraid to take risks around here.

Many organisations have a climate that is downright hostile
towards implementation: a climate that discourages the
creation and execution of great projects. While many of these
organisations talk a good game, and will have words like
innovation, integrity and accountability in their core values,
the truth is that they are geared towards maintaining the status
quo rather than exploring brave new worlds.

Implementation is hard enough without having a climate
that makes it even more difficult, or even dangerous. A key
part of the implementation imperative at an organisational

level is creating an internal climate in the organisation that is conducive to the implementation of great projects.

Once again, as we can see in figure 15.1, this comes down to the three stages of implementation (start, persevere and complete).

Figure 15.1: implementation climate model

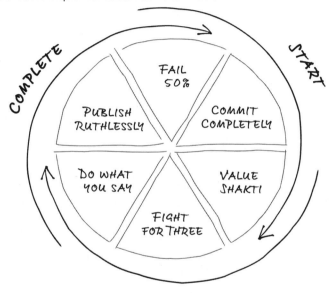

Think about how your organisation handles the three stages of the implementation process—most organisations have strengths and weaknesses across the three. Some organisations aren't good at actually starting projects. There is committee after committee reviewing, revising and revisiting every decision. Several layers of approval are needed. Ideas get diluted, talked about, modified and updated—but rarely executed. Not enough projects get launched.

Guy Kawasaki was marketing strategist at Apple and is now managing director of Garage Technology Ventures. He has written an entire book about this phase of the project—*The Art of the Start*. He focuses on entrepreneurship and provides tips and insights into starting a business from the ground up. However, even though the book is targeted at start-ups, there is a lot that larger organisations can learn, both from start-ups generally, and from this book in particular. Kawasaki talks about 'bootstrapping'—starting a business without external capital—and pitching new ideas to potential investors, but the lessons are valuable for anyone starting any project.

Three of Kawasaki's key recommendations for entrepreneurs are gold for any of us starting a project:

- *Make meaning.* How will your project make the world a better place?

- *Make mantra.* Forget 'long, boring, and irrelevant' mission statements. Instead use a short phrase that is engaging and transformative, capturing the essential function of the organisation. Google's mantra 'Do no evil' is a perfect example of what Kawasaki is talking about.

- *Get going.* Build something. 'Don't focus on pitching, writing, and planning'. Create a prototype, get working on the project—make a start.

While some organisations are weak at starting projects, other organisations are good at starting, but not at persevering. Sometimes it's the risk of failing that makes it safer to jump onto the next project rather than see the current one through. It could be that the resources allocated to implementation are insufficient, and the core business always takes precedence over implementing new ideas, so as soon as it gets tough it's easier to get back to business as usual. Or there just might not be a commitment within the organisation to implementation,

ORGANISATION

and while lip service is paid and things get started, when things get difficult there isn't the fortitude to see it through.

Finally, some organisations aren't good at crossing the finish line. This might be a lack of willingness to declare something a failure, so it's never powerfully completed and is just left to fade away. Perhaps everyone is busy, so that last 10 per cent that would wrap up the project and put it away—or get it launched—never gets done.

As we saw in figure 15.1 (see p. 164), there are things to focus on at each of these three stages to propel our projects forward and to keep the momentum going.

Fail 50 per cent

As we have already seen, at the start of a project we need to embrace the inherent risk of the project failing. Organisations that are great at implementing are also willing to fail, and recognise that failure is a necessary part of success. My good friend and motivation science expert Jason Fox says this beautifully when he writes 'Planning to fail is planning to succeed'—a very clever adaptation of the common adage 'Failing to plan is planning to fail'.

Let me tell you about a recent failure of mine, and I why I think it's so critical that we create a climate within organisations that not only accepts failure, but demands it.

My wife Trish, our newborn Scarlett and I went shopping recently—my first experience in a shopping centre with a baby. We had a list of things that we needed to do, so we thought 'divide and conquer'. I had my half of the list, Trish had her half, and the plan was to meet at a café at the end.

I was taking Scarlett, so Trish asked me if I wanted her to open the pram for me. 'I'll be right', I answered, thinking to myself, 'I've got three degrees. I think I can open a pram.'

Ten minutes later I stopped two women walking past. 'Do you know how to operate this thing? It doesn't look like this when my wife uses it.' One of the women went straight to the magic switch hidden somewhere out of sight, saying, 'Yeah, they're tricky'. Luckily Scarlett had slept through it all rather than cried the whole time.

So I took Scarlett out of the car seat, put her in the pram, and we headed off. Or at least we went to head off, but the hand brake was on. Put me in any car on the planet, and I think I could find the hand brake. But do you think I could find it on the pram? With no-one in the vicinity to help me I was forced to ring Trish (who was already halfway through her list by this time) and ask her what to do.

I believe stuff falls into three categories. You'll want to concentrate here, because I'm about to get technical. The three categories are:

- stuff we can do
- stuff we can't do
- stuff we might be able to do.

Turns out, for me, operating the pram falls into the second category—the stuff I can't do.

The last category is the key to everything. The stuff we *might* be able to do. This is the domain where we have our breakthroughs, where we have our biggest wins, and where we get our biggest learning. This is where innovation lies.

Unfortunately, most organisational climates mean we spend our time in the first category, doing stuff we know that we can do. Not risking the stuff we might be able to do, in case we fail. Not venturing right to the edge of our ability and outside our comfort zone.

ORGANISATION

Creating a climate where failing 50 per cent is encouraged (and, as I said earlier, even required) makes it okay for people to tackle the things they might be able to do, which is critical for tackling projects that matter.

I love the concept of 'organised bravery'. The original purpose of the modern organisation, according to Dee Hock, is to enable the heroic: to make it easy, natural and expected for people to take risks, to lean out of the boat, to be adventurous and human. Hock was the founder of Visa and author of *Birth of the Chaordic Age*. In this ground-breaking work, Dee Hock explains that the first companies were created at the dawn of the 17th century and were designed to allow groups of individuals to do things beyond the scope of an individual or family.

Alas, as marketing guru Seth Godin points out (sethgodin. typepad.com/seths_blog), most organisations today do the opposite. They institutionalise organisational cowardice. They give their people cover, a place to hide, a chance to say 'That's not my job'.

During times of change, the only organisations that thrive are those that are eager to interact and change as well, and that only happens when individuals take brave steps forward and create and execute projects with courage. Giving your team cover for their anxiety is foolish. Give them a platform for bravery instead.

Netflix gives us a great example of doing this well. Netflix Inc is a US-based global provider of on-demand internet streaming media. It is one of the companies that has killed the local video store. As it says on its website, it lets you 'watch TV shows and movies anytime, anywhere'.

At last count Netflix had 23.6 million subscribers in the United States and another 26 million worldwide. The company has global revenues of over US$3 billion. So it is doing all right.

Netflix, as a company, is known as much for its culture as for its innovative business model. As reported on its website, this approach to embracing innovation is known as Netflix's Freedom and Responsibility Culture. The company names nine skills and behaviours that are core to its culture and these apply to employees from the top down. These are: judgement, communication, impact, curiosity, innovation, courage, passion, honesty and selflessness.

Netflix has built a business that is growing rapidly by allowing individuals the freedom to take creative risks without that overwhelming sense of fear or judgment. Employees are encouraged to take risks and this is reflected in the fact that courage is one of the nine core behaviours that should be exhibited by a model employee. Below are the four criteria that underpin courage and risk-taking at Netflix:

- Say what you think, even if it is controversial.

- Make tough decisions without agonising excessively.

- Take smart risks.

- Question actions inconsistent with core values.

As well as encouraging people to take risks, Netflix is also welcoming of mistakes. Under the core value of honesty, it asks that all its employees be 'quick to admit mistakes'.

Incorporating the concept of failing 50 per cent into your organisational climate necessitates taking smart risks. And, ironically, in the long run playing safe is much riskier than taking the right sort of risks, and having the right failures along the way.

The idea of failing 50 per cent helps us to get started — we are much more likely to commence a project that is a bit risky if we know that the organisation accepts and encourages failure. This idea also helps us to complete projects. In organisations where

ORGANISATION

failure isn't accepted, projects will often be left unfinished so that they never have to be declared a failure.

Commit completely

At the start, the most important thing for an organisation to do is to powerfully choose the project, and commit to it completely.

A friend of mine was looking at investing in a business recently, and he asked me to meet the two principals to make an assessment of the business.

One of the questions I asked them was how committed they were to the business. I asked them to rate it out of 10, where one out of 10 was not at all committed, and 10 out of 10 was completely committed — would do whatever it takes.

The two guys answered seven and eight respectively. I was staggered. They were asking someone to back them financially, and their level of commitment was nowhere near what it takes to get a start-up business off the ground.

Of course I told my friend not to go near the business. A new business, like any new project, needs total commitment.

This ties into the first point about embracing risk and being willing to fail. Mostly we don't commit completely because we are scared of failing.

At an organisational level we want the organisation to be committed to lots of projects, even knowing that many, most even, will fail.

General Electric (GE) demonstrated its commitment to implementing projects that matter through the creation of GE Global Research to serve as the hub of technology development for all its businesses. It has created 10 laboratories around the world focused on leveraging technology breakthroughs across multiple GE businesses—in other words, taking things from being great ideas to products that can be sold.

This global research program, and the free time it provides to selected GE employees, has generated many of the company's most successful projects and best-selling products—and has resulted in 580 patents being submitted.

GE invests heavily in developing lots of potential projects, and then powerfully chooses the ones to implement and commits to them completely.

At an organisational level we need to commit completely to the projects we launch. We also need to commit to a culture of implementation, and acknowledge the importance of creating and executing projects that matter for the success, and even survival, of the business.

Value shakti

When I was recently putting together a program on time management and implementation, my dad introduced me to *chronos* and *kairos*, the two words the ancient Greeks used for time.

Chronos refers to chronological or sequential time, while kairos means the right or opportune moment (the supreme moment)—it signifies a time in between, a moment of indeterminate time in which something special happens. What the special something is depends on who is using the word.

Mostly when we think about time management, productivity, efficiency and effectiveness, we are talking about using chronological time, chronos, better. I don't think we pay enough attention to kairos, those critical moments upon which everything turns. Regular productivity is about getting better

ORGANISATION

with chronological time. Implementation is about creating, recognising and taking advantage of critical moments.

And that requires shakti, the concept we have talked about earlier, describing our life force or energy. Valuing shakti means recognising that implementing projects that matter requires more than putting in the time — they need us to bring all of ourselves to our work. And when that happens, critical moments show up, and everything changes.

Organisations need to create a climate that values results over simply putting in the hours, and recognise that it is our shakti, our life force, that produces these results, particularly when implementing projects that matter.

Fight for three

An organisational climate that helps us get through the persevere phase of the project — the tough middle stage — needs simplicity, and three is a great number for that.

An implementation climate rewards results rather than time. And at an individual level within an organisation, having people fight for three meaningful results in a given day is much more productive than asking them to clock in and then clock out eight hours later.

At an organisation level it is also powerful to have three key projects that the organisation as a whole is fighting for. Imagine a board meeting where the CEO acknowledged all the complexity of the organisation, but said that over the next year, or the next quarter, these are the three projects that we are fighting for. It's a different way of running a company — rather than creating a detailed strategic plan and business plan, launch projects that matter. And the ones that work — they become the strategy.

Complexity, bureaucracy and red tape kill implementation in organisations. Fighting for three at all levels counters this influence.

Do what you say

Creating a climate of integrity, a culture where there is congruence between words and actions within an organisation, is critical for implementation.

Implementing projects that matter is hard, because there are many things that will pull a team and an organisation back into the core business. Organisations that have the ability to make commitments and fulfil them will manage to persevere despite these hurdles.

Here are some questions to ask to get a sense of how strong integrity is in an organisation:

- Can the clients trust the promises of the brand and the company?

- Can the staff count on the promises of the leadership?

- Does everyone count on each other?

- Do people take responsibility when things aren't done, or do they look to pass the buck?

Integrity is an espoused value of most organisations. You will see it framed on many walls as a core value. However, it's a lived value in far fewer organisations — but it's critical for creating and executing projects that matter.

Publish ruthlessly

Publish in this context means 'get it out there'. By being ruthless about getting version one out into the world instead of waiting

ORGANISATION

173

for it to be perfect, ruthless publishers show they understand that perfection is the enemy of profit.

Many companies spend millions on research and development, but early-stage marketing can prove a more cost-effective way of developing new products.

When marathon runner Brian Maxwell created PowerBar (an energy food for endurance athletic competition) in 1986 for a few thousand dollars, it received mixed initial reviews. Serious athletes liked it because it met an important need — quick energy during competition — but the taste and consistency was not good.

Maxwell knew that the product wasn't optimal, but by getting feedback on an early version he was able to modify it, and change the packaging and marketing strategy to build a following among athletes and weekend warriors. PowerBar eventually became a $150 million business, creating the $1 billion energy bar category. In 2000, Nestlé bought the brand for about $350 million.

Maxwell's approach of purposefully launching an imperfect product has been adopted by many leading organisations as a new innovation tactic. Rather than making big upfront research and development investment in new ideas, these companies instead start with an MVP, or minimum viable product, a term coined by Eric Ries, author of *The Lean Startup*.

Starbucks is a master of this. Every new product concept — from a new flavour of frappuccino to an updated store design — is tested in a handful of stores while the idea is still new.

When Starbucks launched its line of instant coffee, Via, many pundits questioned whether the product would succeed. They didn't know Via had already survived several rounds of store testing that measured its real sales. From this testing, Starbucks followed up by ensuring it had the right product, package, branding and marketing program. The company knew exactly what to expect from Via, which is now a $180 million brand.

The goal for implementing important projects is not perfection, but faster cycles. That means an implementation climate that encourages getting a version to a point where it's good enough, publishing that ruthlessly, and iterating fast.

IN SUMMARY

The internal climate, or culture, of an organisation is critical to how successful it will be in implementing projects that matter. It is difficult enough to make important projects happen without having to work in a climate that makes implementation harder and even more dangerous to do. At an organisational level, there needs to be a commitment to executing projects that matter, a demand for the right sort of failure, and a premium placed on integrity and completion.

Three things to do

1 Create a strategy to reward failure. Celebrate the right failures as much as you do the successes. Have an award for a noble attempt, or a strategic failure.

2 Determine three key projects that are being implemented at an organisational level, that the organisation is going to fight for. Write them down on one sticky note.

3 Commit the leadership of the organisation to keeping their word and living with integrity at a whole new level to model what is expected throughout the organisation.

Chapter 16
—— PROJECTS ——

The secret of getting ahead is getting started. The secret of getting started is breaking your complex overwhelming tasks into small manageable tasks, and then starting on the first one.

Mark Twain, author

Great organisations implement great projects — it's what makes them great organisations. Of course, other things are also going on all the time — the things that keep the organisation running.

If you look at figure 16.1 (overleaf), showing the organisational projects model, to the left of the line is where the core business lives. From an implementation perspective, all of that is great. It's what pays the bills and provides the resources to pay for the implementation of great projects. Traditional management lives there too — you manage systems by monitoring what happens by when. You manage responses. You can't manage great projects the same way.

The new rules of management mean that we still manage everything to the left of the line, but we recognise that the priority is what's to the right of the line. The priority is implementing projects that matter. But that's not easy.

Figure 16.1: organisational projects model

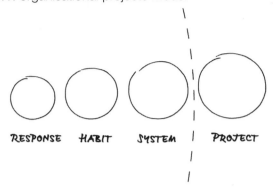

RESPONSE   HABIT   SYSTEM | PROJECT

We said earlier that in 2012 Apple was the most valuable publicly listed company in the world, with a market capitalisation of around US$600 billion. There is actually a privately owned company that's worth about three times that—the only trillion-dollar company in the world. That company is Saudi Aramco, the national oil company of Saudi Arabia, owned by the Saudi royal family.

Saudi Aramco called us up a couple of years ago with an interesting problem. It had a database of 100 000 ideas, submitted by its staff over the last decade, that it didn't know what to do with. Ten years earlier it had launched an innovation initiative, and asked its 50 000–odd staff to submit ideas for what they could do better. It had received lots of ideas and wanted help making them happen. So I went across to Saudi Arabia to work with a bunch of its leaders to work out how to implement some of these ideas.

The problem was that it really doesn't need to create growth. It is sitting on the world's biggest oilfield. It basically turns a tap and pumps a billion dollars worth of oil a day. That takes a bit of getting your head around. In Australia there aren't too many companies that make a billion dollars a year. Saudi Aramco makes a billion dollars *a day*. And that is just by running its existing systems and responding to external demand. It doesn't need to implement any great projects to make that happen.

So imagine someone in Saudi Aramco had submitted an idea that could make $10 million—which most of us would be pretty happy with. And imagine it takes a quarter of an hour to read the business case: in that quarter of an hour it had just pumped $10 million worth of oil. So it could go to all the effort of implementing this $10 million idea, or it could just wait another 15 minutes.

The challenge for Saudi Aramco is that going from having an idea to executing a project is hard, and there is no imperative for the company to do so. Time will tell whether the work we did will lead to real change, or things will just go back to business as usual.

In your business, selling your existing products to your existing market using your existing systems is like using your existing oilfield. Implementing projects that matter is like finding new oilfields or new energy sources. And that is something that most companies do really badly.

Response

A lot of time and energy in our organisations is spent responding to internal and external stimuli. This is as it should be—we need to respond to a customer making an order, or an opportunity that presents itself, or a change in our environment. Our organisations are part of a wider ecosystem, and we need to respond to changes within that.

There is also a lot of response required internally—within the organisation we need to respond to those senior to us, to our peers and to members of our team.

ORGANISATION

Typically, responding is the easiest level to operate at. And the trap is that it is easy to spend all our time responding to urgent demands on our time, and never making the time to create and execute the projects that matter. We can spend a day (or a week, or a year, or even a career) answering emails, attending meetings, putting out fires, responding to requests and feeling very busy, but without ever creating anything that matters.

Habit

There are things that are done habitually within an organisation. The culture of an organisation — the way things are done around here — could be described as the habits of an organisation.

And as with personal habits, organisational habits are easy to follow, but they're even harder to change. It is worth looking at the habits of your organisation, and determining whether they support or undermine the implementation of projects that matter.

Systems

I love systems. When I started my career as a management consultant with Accenture, I was in process competency, which basically meant I helped organisations to optimise their processes and systematise them. I'm a big fan of Michael Hammer's work on the management theory that he co-founded, which he called process re-engineering, a term that has become part of the business lexicon.

I believe a big part of the value of any organisation is its systems. There is incredible power in being able to map out an end-to-end system, be it the entire customer experience or any other complete system in a business, and find ways to improve it.

As a business coach working with small businesses, part of my focus has always been to create world-class systems. One client, Debbie Roberts, did such a good job of that in her bookkeeping business that we got to a point where I told her that her systems were so good that I thought she would make more money selling her systems to other bookkeeping businesses than she would bookkeeping. We have since created a business together to do that, and her systems are now being used by bookkeeping businesses across Australia, and now the UK, too, and have become the standard for best practice bookkeeping in Australia.

So I'm a fan of systems. Yet what I am about to say might seem sacrilegious to most systems engineers and process experts.

The point of great systems is that they free us up to focus on projects that matter. Organisations that don't have great systems in place need all their thinking, time and energy, all their shakti, to run their core business. There is nothing left for projects.

Projects

Because projects are hard, and risky, the organisation needs to carve out time and money to make them happen, and that's a commitment that has worked well for several market leaders, as we saw for GE in chapter 15.

Atlassian, an Australian software company, does this really well. It has what it calls FedEx days two or three times a year. During these days everyone has 24 hours to deliver something great. They are called FedEx days because of the FedEx slogan 'We deliver'. There's even a trophy for the most innovative project. In 2011, blogs.atlassian.com reported:

> Every quarter, we give employees the chance to work on anything that relates to our products, and deliver it within 24 hours—hence the name, FedEx Day. Been wanting to build that plugin, redesign that interface, or completely rethink that feature that's been bugging you? You've got 24 hours … go!

ORGANISATION

This program has been so successful for Atlassian that it has been copied by other leading companies.

Some companies, such as Google, formally budget project time into job descriptions and ultimately into employee time, and this is called '20 per cent time'. While there's no concrete definition of 20 per cent time, the general understanding is that engineers (any employee with a technical or development role) work the equivalent of one day a week on their own, researching individual projects that the company funds and supports, with the only expectation being these projects have the potential to benefit Google in some way.

The Google products to have come out of 20 per cent time projects include Gmail, Google News, Google Talk and AdSense.

Living to the right of the line (see figure 16.1, p. 178) requires a commitment to investing in a project mindset. Google is another example of a company that gets this, and it comes out in its publicity, its language and how it balances its time.

In my mind, every revenue stream in a business started out as a project that mattered. The product, or service, or alliance, started out as a great idea. That idea became a project — and was implemented. Once the project was proven it was scaled, and then became part of the core business. It moved from the right of the line to the left of the line.

Traditional management is all about how to optimise the revenue streams to the left of the line, how to keep them going and make them as efficient as possible. The new rules of management require us to fight for resources, time, energy and attention on the right-hand side of the line. Our core business still needs to be great, and that's what makes us profit and also what funds our projects that matter. But our future revenue streams all start out as projects on the right of the line. And organisations that aren't investing there are sacrificing the future for immediate profit, and dooming themselves to failure when their existing revenue streams dry up.

IN SUMMARY

As with individuals and teams, it's easier for an organisation to live on the left of the line (see figure 16.1, p. 178). That's where the core business, the existing turnover and the profit lives. Moving to the right of the line feels more dangerous, and it means trading some short-term profit for long-term success.

Of course the safety on the left of the line is an illusion. All products have a life cycle. If you aren't creating something new, no matter how good your habits or systems are, the organisation will eventually perish.

Three things to do

1 Document the three key projects that the organisation is embarking on, using a one-page template which you can download at www.newrulesofmanagement.com. Even at an organisational level, you should be able to describe these projects on one page.

2 Determine the resources that the organisation is currently committing to projects that matter. Then increase this amount substantially.

3 Create some dedicated implementation time for your organisation, whether it's modelled on Atlassian's FedEx Days or Google's 20 per cent time, or something else entirely.

Chapter 17

—— FRAMEWORK ——

Vision without action is a daydream.
Action without vision is a nightmare.

Japanese proverb

All our projects, and everything that we implement, sit within an overall framework. The framework answers the questions why we implement, where we do it, and how. It's made up of our context, our environment and our method.

The implementation framework model (figure 17.1, overleaf) shows how the different elements of our framework — the context, environment and method — fit together. It also shows what happens at the intersections of these three elements. The implementation framework is even more important at the organisational level than with our teams or individually — at an organisational level the framework has a much bigger impact. Get this wrong in one team, and the team will suffer. But get it wrong at an organisational level, and the whole business could be crippled.

Figure 17.1: implementation framework model

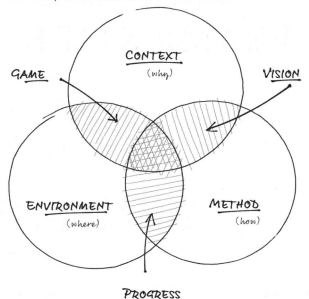

Context: why

Context is all about the why of any project. It includes the purpose for the organisation, and its mission and vision.

Google has had a very clear context since its inception in 1998: 'to organise the world's information and make it universally accessible and useful'. It's its reason for being, and that has made it very easy for Google to decide if a project fits its context. The vision for any project needs to fit into the overall organisational context. A clear context makes it easy to decide what is core to the project and organisational vision and what is not.

Back in the 1990s IBM was struggling. Against the backdrop of the rise of Silicon Valley, which was seen as the epicentre of innovation in the technology sector, IBM was beginning to look oversized and decrepit. Talented IT folk were heading in their droves to the small, high-growth companies in Silicon Valley, because they saw these companies implementing great projects that they wanted to be part of. It was now time for IBM to strike back.

IBM's solution was to build BlueGene. The vision: to build the fastest computer in the world with groundbreaking underlying technologies. In a 1999 press conference, IBM announced that it would invest $100 million over five years in a new machine, to be dubbed BlueGene, that would be the fastest computer in the world.

Super computers at that time were operating at speeds of about one teraflop; the technical definition of a teraflop is a trillion floating point operations per second, or, as I like to think of it, really, really fast. Apparently, though, not fast enough for some. Some scientific research was limited by the speed at which computers could process calculations. IBM set out to make a computer that could operate at 1 petaflop, which is technically 1000 times faster, and what I call really, really, really, really fast (apologies if I'm being too technical here). A computer that fast would empower the world of scientific endeavour by allowing a whole new class of calculations to be processed. By 2004, BlueGene was running at over 36 teraflops and was the fastest computer in the world. BlueGene broke the petaflop barrier in 2007.

Establishing such a groundbreaking challenge not only forced IBM to implement projects in ways it had never done before, it also allowed it to once again attract some of the world's most talented graduate students, who will in turn lead to great future innovation at IBM.

ORGANISATION

It also created a powerful new context for IBM. If you worked at IBM at that time, you were working at the company that was building the world's fastest computer. The 1999 press conference, and the goal of making a computer 1000 times faster, was the corporate equivalent of President John F. Kennedy announcing in 1961 that the United States would put a man on the moon by the turn of the decade.

Environment: where

The aim of creating an environment that helps us implement projects that matter is to create a space that is not only highly productive, but also conducive to implementing great projects. A productive environment takes into account the tools, space, colour, stimulus and electronic environments required to complete a project.

Web developer Paul Stamatiou's article about Yahoo! (www. paulstamatiou.com/a-look-inside-yahoo-brickhouse) gives us a good example of creating an environment for implementation.

Within Silicon Valley, Yahoo!, the multinational internet corporation built on its early success with the search engine Yahoo! Search, had a reputation for being bureaucratic and slow to innovate, especially in contrast to rival Google. To infuse itself with start-up energy — read implementation energy — in 2007 Yahoo set up an offsite incubator called Brickhouse. The brief to staff at Brickhouse was to shorten the time it takes to bring new ideas to market.

While the main Yahoo! office remained in Silicon Valley, Brickhouse was located in the South of Market district, a hip neighbourhood in nearby San Francisco.

Brickhouse generated and implemented successful products such as Pipes, a free software tool that lets users gather and mix RSS feeds from many websites; and Fire Eagle, a web-based software platform that lets people meet up with co-workers and friends more easily by broadcasting their whereabouts, often tracked by GPS, in online posts or cell-phone text messages. Fire Eagle took only three months to develop—about 65 per cent less time than the fastest development of typical Yahoo products.

Brickhouse demonstrates the importance of environment to implementation, and that Yahoo! had the foresight to recognise this. In a way Brickhouse did the job of replicating the environment of a start-up too well: a string of leaders from Brickhouse left Yahoo! to join start-ups, which eventually lead to Yahoo! shutting down the facility.

We almost always underestimate the impact that our environment has on us, and it is worth investing in making the physical space that the organisation operates in conducive to implementing projects that matter.

Method: how

A big failure point in implementing new projects is the methodology—how to go about getting projects done. The approach to tackling a new, innovative project is very different to the one applied to business as usual. The final part of the organisational framework for implementation is how the organisation treats the process of creating and executing the work that really matters.

Deloitte Digital was created in Australia in 2010 with Deloitte partner Pete Williams as its CEO. Its purpose was to become the 'Amazon.com of professional services'. Pete explained it to me: 'As a professional services firm we were in the business of trading time for money. We wanted to work out how to make money while we slept ... through selling stuff online.'

ORGANISATION

In other words, Deloitte was like a traditional professional services firm: they were in the business of selling the time of their consultants. Deloitte Digital was set up to turn that business model on its head and start to make money from some of the great ideas their people came up with, by creating online products that could be sold time and time again.

The basic methodology is very simple. Deloitte Australia runs an innovation program which collects ideas from its people either through an online tool or via Idea Cafes and Design Thinking Workshops. The ideas are reviewed by an Innovation Council made up of people from across all areas of Deloitte. Of the ideas submitted around 70 per cent relate to digitising services or creating new digital service offerings; the ones that merit it are awarded A$10 000 in microfunding and given 90 days to produce a prototype. After 90 days the prototype is evaluated, and at that point the projects are abandoned, or given another round of microfunding, or scaled more aggressively.

This approach has been so successful in Australia that after only two years it has gone global, with the creation of a new global business unit focused on digital media and employing close to 1000 people. In addition, a network of nine digital studios in the United States, the United Kingdom and Australia has been launched.

The implementation methodology developed by Williams and his team was heavily influenced by venture capital firm Y-Combinator. While most venture capital funds place a few big bets after lots of due diligence, Y-Combinator has taken the approach of making many smaller bets. Its model is to give start-ups on average US$18 000, give them 90 days to see how far they get, and then re-assess. It has proved incredibly successful: since 2005 more than 460 start-ups have been funded, including household names like Dropbox, Reddit and Bump. *Wired Magazine* called its finding program 'the most prestigious program for budding entrepreneurs'.

The Deloitte Digital approach has been equally successful. Adam Powick, leader of Deloitte Consulting in Australia, said in *iTWire*: 'The strength of the Deloitte Digital and Online practices in Australia has been a key contributor to Deloitte Consulting's rapid growth rate and has paved the way for this global initiative. Peter Williams ... did an outstanding job.'

This is definitely a methodology worth stealing. Much better to place lots of small bets, and launch lots of projects, than go all out on a few that haven't been tested at all. It turns out that, with businesses, it's better to get them spending 90 days building a prototype than spending 90 days writing a 150-page business plan. Likewise within our organisations, better to allocate $10 000 to get a prototype developed, and determine the commitment of the team, than it is to spend $1 million based on a business case (after all, there's never been a business case written that doesn't make money ...). Out of the 100 projects that we could launch for the same $1 million, we are going to get a much better return from making small bets.

Game

At the intersection of context and environment in the model shown in figure 17.1 (see p. 186) is game—the idea that the more the project feels like a game, and the more it has the energy of play, the more likely it is to succeed.

There is an entire movement in organisational psychology around game design. Behavioural scientists have realised that people spend hours and hours of discretionary time in game environments doing stuff that looks a lot like work.

The World Bank–sponsored Evoke game, which crowd-sources ideas from players around the world to solve social challenges, is a good example of implementing game design in a project. Wanting to educate people, and come up with specific solutions

ORGANISATION

to third-world rural challenges, the World Bank didn't create a typical media campaign, or scour universities for experts to engage. Instead they engaged alternative reality game master Jane McGonigal to build them an online game, and Evoke (www.urgentevoke.net) was the result. Almost 20 000 players from around the world joined the first round of the game in 2010, being educated and contributing real world solutions.

As motivational science and game-design expert Jason Fox says:

> The benefit of viewing organisational implementation through the lens of game design is that you're simultaneously driving progress while maintaining engagement. It's a pragmatic and agile approach to improvement making and effective work.
>
> When done well, games provide opportunities to manage context and instill epic meaning in the work you do, as well as provide an environment that facilitates blissful productivity and an urgent optimism for progress-making.

Good game design enables us to do great work without feeling like it's work. A frightening number of people spend an inordinate amount of time playing complex online games, doing stuff that looks a lot like work, for free, and for fun. It makes sense to incorporate as much of that into our organisations' projects as we can, to lift engagement, productivity and fun.

Progress

At the intersection of context and method, in the model shown in figure 17.1 (see p. 186), lies progress. As we saw in chapter 11, progress is the primary motivator for employees to engage in their work and provide discretionary effort.

One of the main reasons that we find long-term projects difficult is that we are wired to seek short-term pleasure. A task that takes two minutes and gives us a little hit of satisfaction is more attractive than the idea of spending time on a long-term project, which only gives us a benefit down the road.

An experience of progress takes something that is beneficial in the long term, and gives us short-term pleasure. In our organisations, we need to build in progress feedback within our projects to keep people focused and to keep projects moving.

IBM's transformation into a project-based business has taken years; in fact, IBM invested 15 years making project implementation the focus for driving growth and successful business results. Let's look at what prompted this new approach.

In the mid 1990s IBM was in a world of trouble. After dominating first the mainframe and then the personal computer (PC) industries through the 1980s, things were falling apart. The PC revolution had slashed mainframe computer sales, and despite an early lead in the PC market IBM had been passed by most of their serious competitors. Between 1991 and 1993 the company posted net losses of almost US$16 billion, including a US$8.2 billion dollar loss in 1992, a single-year record in the United States at the time. The computer industry viewed IBM as an irrelevant dinosaur. The IBM workforce was almost halved from more than 400 000 down to 220 000 in 1994.

Against this backdrop the new CEO at the time, Louis Gerstner, decided to transform IBM into a project-based enterprise. As technology website www.techcrunch.com reports, IBM has achieved this transformation by delivering the following five areas of focus:

- a consistent project management delivery approach across IBM
- qualified project managers are assigned to all significant projects

ORGANISATION

193

- project managers and business executives are rewarded for project and business success

- the development and nurturing of a committed, vibrant project management community

- re-use of project management knowledge, experiences and best practices.

One focus of its attention was using both recognition and reward in project management. Project managers and business executives at IBM are accountable for project and business success through the use of consistent project performance measurements and metrics. In other words, progress is monitored, measured and rewarded.

IBM has successfully averted disaster and is once again a leading global brand in the IT world. Indeed, we covered one of IBM's successful projects in chapter 11 — the development of the supercomputer that won *Jeopardy*.

There are two lessons to draw from this. The first is the importance of focusing on implementing projects, and how critical the decision to make that change was to the survival of IBM. The second lesson is the importance of incorporating progress measures into your project methodology. Make sure that each project has milestones and progress points that are measured, recognised and rewarded.

Vision

The framework model in figure 17.1 (see p. 186) shows that vision sits at the intersection of context and method.

An example of the power of a clear vision comes from software engineer Linus Torvalds, who created the Linux operating system kernel for Intel personal computers, first released on 5 October 1991. His vision for the project was to create a world-class operating system built as open-source software, and available for free. Linux became one of the most prominent examples of free and open-source software collaboration: the underlying source code could be used, modified, and distributed — commercially or noncommercially — by anyone under a range of licences. The Linux operating system was developed, updated and maintained with the help of a vibrant, passionate and dedicated community of volunteer programmers, the number of which stretched into the thousands. They were not paid for this work; they came together purely out of a sense of belief and purpose in the work and its value for their own projects, inspired by Torvalds's vision.

Torvalds himself continues to coordinate the project through the Linux Foundation and has the final authority over which code becomes incorporated into the standard Linux kernel and systems. Although the additions and modifications now come largely from the corporate sector, Torvalds has been the inspiration for the software that has now been ported to more hardware platforms than any other and is the operating system of choice for 90 per cent of today's 500 fastest computers.

In 2000 Torvalds was named 17th on the *Time* magazine list of the 100 most important people of the 20th century.

The thousands of programmers who maintain and develop Linux volunteer their time for free. They are attracted by Torvalds's vision and the opportunity to solve problems by working together informally on programming and application projects. They are not motivated by money, but by the opportunity to do important work on a project that matters. And the vision that Torvalds painted nearly 30 years ago was what drew these thousands of developers to the project.

When creating your project, paint a clear vision to inspire all the participants, and so everyone is clear and on the same page about what the objective is and what success looks like.

ORGANISATION

IN SUMMARY

In your organisation, creating and communicating your project's context, shaping the environment and developing clear processes or methods to implement projects, provides a shared framework that guides the why, how and where of everything we do. Setting the framework in place is as important for the success of the project as having the right people working on it.

Three things to do

1   Create a project methodology for your organisation, and appoint someone to be accountable for it.

2   Document the purpose for the three key projects the organisation is fighting for, and ensure that they are congruent with the organisation's purpose and values.

3   Imagine you were designing the environment to support the three key projects being implemented, rather than to support business as usual. What would be different? Make one significant change to the environment in that direction.

Chapter 18

──── SUPPORT ────

The greatest glory of leading lies not in never falling,
but in rising every time you fall.

Nelson Mandela, civil rights leader

At an organisational level, it's critical to have a support structure in place to empower and facilitate the implementation of great projects. This means helping the people and the teams who are doing the important work by having their front, having their back, and assisting them with the doing (walking the walk) and the conversations (talking the talk).

Once again our support model (figure 18.1, overleaf) is broken up into doing and talking, and front and back. The four elements of the model at an organisational level are expertise, protection, resourcing and advocacy.

Figure 18.1: organisation support model

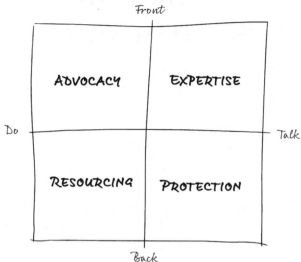

Expertise

The expertise quadrant is about providing advice and know-how that drives results. By its very nature, implementing great, innovative, exciting projects means doing things that are new, unfamiliar and unknown. One of the most powerful support structures to enable this is the provision of expertise (see figure 18.1).

Expertise can come in the form of an internal mentor — someone within the organisation who knows the terrain a bit better, or has experience within the domain. Equally, expertise could come from external advice. This requires the organisation to be willing to recognise that the project is outside its current capability, and that it needs to bring some expertise in. External advice can come through consultants, academic experts and even through crowdsourcing.

An example of the use of external advice comes from US company Procter & Gamble (P&G), which boasts boatloads of top household brands. It is the world's largest maker of consumer packaged goods; it owns about two dozen brands that are are billion-dollar sellers, including Braun, Gillette, Head & Shoulders (worth a billion dollars—who would have thought?), Olay, Oral-B, Duracell, and Tide. At the turn of the 21st century Procter & Gamble operated one of the greatest research and development operations in corporate history. But as the company grew to a $70 billion enterprise, the innovation model it devised in the 1980s was no longer up to the task.

Larry Huston and Nabil Sakkab, P&G vice president and senior vice president, respectively, wrote about their Connect and Develop strategy in the March 2006 *Harvard Business Review*:

> It was clear to us that our invent-it-ourselves model was not capable of sustaining high levels of top-line growth. Our R&D productivity had leveled off, and our innovation success rate—the percentage of new products that met financial objectives—had stagnated at about 35 percent … we lost more than half our market cap [the total value of the company] when our stock slid from $118 to $52 a share. Talk about a wake-up call.

In response to the loss, in 2001 P&G created its Connect and Develop strategy, which has transformed its traditional in-house research and development process into what it describes as an open-source innovation platform. Under this strategy P&G contracts with a broad spectrum of partners for specific initiatives. The partners may be research organisations, suppliers, inventors, joint venture organisations,

ORGANISATION

even competitors. The partnerships each achieve one or more of the following objectives:

- enable innovation beyond the specific expertise within P&G
- provide access to existing innovative ideas that have not yet been commercialised
- share the risks in innovation
- allow complementary collaboration with the resources of other organisations.

Using this open-source platform allows the organisation to embrace the collective brains of the world to identify new products that can be developed, manufactured and marketed through these partnerships. P&G's initial goal of sourcing 50 per cent of the company's new products from outside its own laboratories — from external expertise — was surpassed in 2008.

And the share price of P&G has responded, more than doubling since the initiative. In 2011 *Fortune* magazine ranked P&G fifth in a list of the world's most admired companies.

Starbucks is another example of a company that brought in external expertise to help it solve internal problems. Starbucks' ongoing challenge is to figure out how to continue to make innovative products that will appeal to consumers in a highly saturated market. To do this, it has to be sensitive to the changing tastes, desires and whims of its customer base. Rather than adopting the traditional market research and product development process, in 2008 it chose the more innovative method of gaining consumer insight and understanding through its crowd sourcing platform, which is called My Starbucks Idea.

Through this website consumers can share their ideas on products, in-store experiences and customer service. The platform allows customers to make suggestions, vote on suggestions and discuss their ideas. Starbucks can watch all of this activity and observe which ideas gain the most support, and tune its product and service offerings to suit customer needs.

So far, Starbucks has effectively used the wisdom of crowds as an external advice medium to help it develop a more market-oriented offering. An extraordinary 70000 ideas were submitted through the site. Starbucks has successfully crowd-sourced dozens of successful products to date. A few of the ideas the currently in use that came from Starbucks' fans include:

- free coffee for Gold Card members on their birthday
- Starbucks VIP card
- splash sticks, which prevent coffee spurting from the holes in cup lids
- buy coffee beans, get a free cup of coffee.

The 'not invented here syndrome'—the idea that the only valuable ideas come from within the organisation—is arrogant and foolish, and will cripple the implementation of important projects. Be willing to find expertise outside the organisation, and be proactive in doing so.

Protection

With protection we want to provide an environment that enables taking entrepreneurial risks. The energy needed for implementing projects that matter is much more akin to how we think an entrepreneurial start-up behaves than a large organisation. We need to have the same tolerance of risk with our new projects as an entrepreneurial venture does.

ORGANISATION

The people involved with these projects in an organisation need protection. They need protection from the pull of 'business as usual', from the tasks that will bring revenue now and demand that we drop everything and run. They need the protection of knowing that it's okay, and even expected, for projects to fail; that as many will fail as succeed; and that it's part of the game.

Google is one company that understands the value of entrepreneurial risk-taking. It takes aggressive steps to retain employees, particularly those who have start-up ambitions. Google has given several engineers who were on the verge of leaving to start their own companies the chance to start them within Google. These engineers work independently of Google, but can recruit other engineers and use Google's resources, such as its code base and servers. Google is currently considering creating a start-up incubator to protect new ideas and risk-taking behaviour.

The Tata Group is a multinational conglomerate headquartered in Mumbai, India, with more than 100 operating companies in areas as diverse as steel production, car manufacturing, chemicals, communications, beverages and hotels. *The Economist* published an extended report about the company on 3 March 2011, arguing that, while the Tata Group may not be well known for its innovation and risk-taking culture, the recent success of this global conglomerate has been built on a risk-taking environment carefully cultivated over the past five years through the following four main initiatives:

- Tata has developed formal systems through which employees can raise ideas and the most promising ideas can be identified, funded and taken forwards. This involves communicating with employees and ensuring that they know who to take innovative ideas to. The company requires that the 'go to' person has an organisational process to move the idea forward. Multiple upward communication channels were created, and funding for innovative projects was built into the company budget.

- Tata employees are allowed to devote up to five hours a week to develop a new idea.

- Tata encourages and recognises innovation through its annual group-wide competition, recognising both Successful Innovations and Failed Experiments. The latter award is to ensure that an environment is created where employees feel comfortable taking risks. Tata wanted to show that both failure and risk-taking are part of the innovation process.

- The company also established a Young Innovator Award, which leads to both a financial reward and an increased likelihood of fast-track career progression.

The Tata Group does a great job of protecting employees who are implementing the projects that matter, and provides an environment where risk-taking is safe, and even encouraged.

Resourcing

It's critical for organisations to provide the resources—the time, money and people—to fulfil their projects. Many organisations pay lip service to implementation, to the creation and execution of innovative projects, but when the rubber hits the road and it's time to resource them, nothing happens. However, as CNN's Money website reported on 23 September 2010, 3M is not one of those companies.

3M is a multinational conglomerate based in Minnesota, United States. It is known popularly for its adhesives, but it manufactures more than 55 000 products. The company

ORGANISATION

discovered that its group and department managers were focused on core-related projects, and didn't want to spend money on exploring or developing innovative ideas. 3M believes that an effective way to overcome this common roadblock is to establish an alternative source of funds, which employees can go to for funding innovative projects that don't fit neatly into existing departments: 3M calls these Genesis Grants.

Each year more than 60 researchers submit formal applications to a panel of 20 senior scientists who review the requests, just as a foundation would review academic proposals. Twelve to 20 grants, ranging from $50000 to $100000 each, are awarded each year. The researchers can use the money to hire additional staff or acquire necessary equipment. 3M has also awarded Genesis Grants to scientists who want to work on outside projects.

As the venture funded by a Genesis Grant achieves certain revenue goals, the team members receive raises, promotions and recognition. For example, the Golden Step Award is given if a new product is launched and reaches a revenue goal of $2 million in the United States or $4 million worldwide. Products generated from these initiatives include Scotch pop-up tape and the 3M multilayer optical film for laptop and cellular phone displays.

The new rules of management dictate a whole new level of resourcing for innovative projects. And the organisations that are experiencing the most success in the 21st century are the ones that are putting their money where their mouth is when it comes to implementing projects that matter.

Advocacy

The final element of support at the organisational level is advocacy—championing the project both internally and externally.

American mobile phone company T-Mobile is an organisation that has almost industrialised this process of championing projects, and has done so to great effect. In 2009 T-Mobile introduced an Enterprise Program Office (EPO). Its charter was to advocate for the projects that matter, making sure they had what they needed to succeed.

The focus of the EPO has been on program and project delivery—managing projects from inception to completion, in partnership with the sponsors who initiated the projects. By putting into practice effective project advocacy, as well as change management and governance, the team has improved the project success rate at T-Mobile.

I think this is a great initiative from T-Mobile. The role of advocating for projects, championing them both internally and externally, is often overlooked. It can be the critical piece that makes the difference between success and failure. By creating an office with this exact charter, T-Mobile shows that it gets it, that it values the implementation of projects and is committed to giving these projects the support they need.

ORGANISATION

--------------- IN SUMMARY ---------------

Implementing projects that matter is difficult and risky. We need to recognise how critical they are for the success and survival of our organisation, and to start giving them the support they deserve. This can mean finding appropriate external expertise, as Procter & Gamble have done so successfully; providing the protection required to make risk-taking safe, as we saw Google and the Tata group demonstrate; providing the necessary resources, like 3M does; and, of course, providing advocacy in the way T-Mobile does.

Three things to do

1   Increase the amount of resources, time and money that is committed to implementing projects that matter in the organisation.

2   For the three key projects being implemented within the organisation, find one key external expert to assist each project.

3   Encourage the senior leaders within the organisation to always act as an advocate for at least one important project that matters to them and to the business.

Chapter 19
– ACCOUNTABILITY –

Leadership is the serious meddling in the lives of others.
To earn the right of that type of meddling, above all
leadership is a position of servanthood, and integrity is the
lynchpin of this leadership. Furthermore in a special
way all the qualities of a good leader stem from an
awareness of the human spirit.

Max Dupree, former CEO of Herman Miller Corporation

Different levels of accountability are like a currency we have in our organisations (see figure 19.1, overleaf). There are some things we leave up to people's private accountability. Sometimes peer accountability is enough. Often there is positional accountability, typically where a person or team reports to someone at a higher level in the organisation; and sometimes there is public accountability—accountability to the whole organisation or beyond.

The IBM BlueGene project, to create a supercomputer 1000 times faster than the fastest computer of the day (discussed in chapter 17), is a great example of creating public accountability, because the company announced its plans in a press conference. It made it much harder for it to give up when the going got tough.

Figure 19.1: accountability model

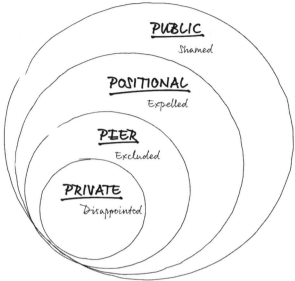

The thing about the different levels of accountability is that each currency is finite. There are only a few things that you can declare publicly or organisation-wide to make use of public accountability. If IBM had declared 173 different strategic initiatives at the press conference, the strategy wouldn't have worked. No-one would remember or care, and the point of the exercise would have been lost.

Likewise there are only a limited number of things that an employee can be held accountable for by his or her boss. The key is to recognise that projects that matter are hard enough and important enough to use this currency on.

Private

Private accountability is at the level of personal responsibility, and FedEx uses this level effectively. Much of FedEx's high reputation around delivery—it lives up to its motto 'we deliver'—can be attributed to its employees' creativity, and their ideas and strategies help to build the business and keep customers satisfied.

Through the development of a company-wide management style, FedEx created a work environment that encourages employee dedication, innovation and creativity. This management style is based on the company's core philosophy—people–service–profit. In other words, the company takes care of its people so they can provide impeccable service to its clients, who will deliver the profit back to the company.

One of the key tenets of this philosophy is private accountability. If any employee of FedEx sees something that needs to be done to look after a customer, they are expected to do it. Not to check with their boss to see if they should do it, not to wait until whoever's job it is to do it, but to actually step in and take the action. Every employee is accountable to themselves, first, to do this.

There are some things within your organisation, and your projects, that are best left at the private accountability level. Things that don't need to be put into job descriptions or status meetings, but that the staff are trusted to look after themselves.

Peer

In chapter 13 we talked about Atlassian's FedEx Days, and how the Atlassian team uses peer accountability to implement innovative projects over a 24-hour period once every few months. Dan Pink, best-selling author and journalist (and one-time chief speech writer for former US Vice President Al Gore) mentioned Atlassian, and this process, in a 10-minute video he did called *Drive – The Surprising Truth About What Motivates Us*. The video has gone viral, with more than 10 million views, and it has made Atlassian's FedEx Days famous.

So much so that Atlassian has now started exporting these 'hack days' to other organisations around the world. As part of this they have renamed their days 'ShipIt' days—I'm guessing FedEx would eventually get unhappy about its name being appropriated.

Atlassian ran a competition offering the winner's prize of sending three of their ShipIt experts to run a day just for you, bringing all their expertise, a trophy, a bunch of T-shirts and a keg of beer (because, as they say, all ShipIt days go better with beer). Nintendo in the US won the competition (as reported on Atlassian's website) and I love what Dave Tempero, the director of the infrastructure and operations teams at Nintendo, said about it:

> Since I first read about ShipIt days, I've realized that would be a good way to spark the creativity I know is within my teams. The benefits to my company however are really just the by products of a much more important change—the spark of excitement and commitment that comes when people are working on projects that they are excited about and fully vested in.

He's hit the nail on the head—*the spark of excitement and commitment that comes when people are working on projects that they are excited about and fully vested in*. Projects that matter. It's why peer accountability works so well on these days. When you let people choose the projects that they want to work on—the projects that are important to them, that they are excited about—you don't have to make them work. All you need to do is give them the opportunity and the space to go to work, and then get out of their way. Let them work together, impress their peers and come up with something great.

Positional

Amy Radin became one of America's first chief innovation officers when Citigroup appointed her to the role in 2005. She is currently chief innovation officer at E*Trade Financial, a leading online discount stock brokerage. Amy's journey is an excellent example of the power of positional authority.

According to businessweek.com in 2006, Amy had a background in direct marketing and product development, and was asked by the CEO of Citi Cards North America to 'help make the business more innovative'. Amy started a 'skunkworks' team within the department she was leading at the time, which focused on identifying and piloting innovative concepts that could represent new opportunities for the business. Amy defined the team's remit around piloting disruptive bets and establishing an innovation portfolio. She also focused on establishing and enabling capabilities that would accelerate innovation potential across the business units, including process, tools, training and more. Her job soon evolved into the role of global consumer chief innovation officer.

At E*Trade, Amy conducts innovation workshops around the company, introducing new techniques for developing ideas, demonstrating through a hands-on exercise that everyone (not just the 'creative types') can play a role in building innovative new businesses, and encouraging open dialogue about how employees can help. For example, Amy created an innovation presence on the corporate intranet where tools and useful public domain materials are made available so people who are interested can build knowledge. The goal is to make it easier for employees to contribute and share ideas, and also

ORGANISATION

to acknowledge innovation, leadership and results through company-wide recognition programs.

Positional accountability is often the default in organisations — we are accountable to our boss, or someone in a position of authority. The key with positional accountability is not to overuse it. If private or peer accountability is sufficient, use that. When everything is run at a positional level, it stops feeling supportive and starts feeling authoritarian. Remember, the point of accountability within a project is to support the people implementing and improve their chances of success, not to make them resentful. Relying too much on positional authority in an organisation is like trying to crack a walnut with a sledgehammer — messy and counterproductive.

Public

Public accountability is perhaps the most risky accountability level for an organisation.

In chapter 18 we looked at Procter & Gamble's Connect and Develop program as a great example of providing external expertise to projects. It's also a great illustration of public accountability. You will recall that in 2001 P&G launched Connect and Develop, a company-wide open innovation program charged with bringing the outside in, and taking the inside out. At the time P&G publicly declared its goal of ensuring 50 per cent of its innovation would contain a significant component of external collaboration. It was a bold move from a company that had spent a century refining its internal research and development labs.

P&G has achieved its original goal, with more than 50 per cent of P&G innovation currently fuelled by external partnership.

By seeking to become the partner of choice for other leading companies, and stating this publicly, P&G has set the bar high and made public accountability part of their brand strategy—a gutsy move that has paid off. It has forced them to go the extra mile, because no-one at P&G wants to be responsible for any project failing.

General Electric (GE) provides another great example of using public accountability to great effect. CEO Jeff Immelt has made the need to generate and execute blockbuster ideas publicly more than an abstract concept. In true GE fashion, he has developed a quantifiable and scalable process for implementing money-making projects that matter. He created the Commercial Council, consisting of 12 top sales and marketing executives, including some unit heads, such as the head of GE Consumer Finance. These members hold phone meetings every month and meet each quarter to discuss growth strategies, think up ways to reach customers, and evaluate ideas from the senior ranks that aim to take GE out on a limb.

Internal business leaders must submit at least three Imagination Breakthrough proposals each year, which go before the council for review and discussion. The projects, which will receive billions in funding in future years, have to take GE into a new line of business, geographic area, or customer base and deliver an incremental growth of at least $100 million.

Since the program began in mid 2003, Immelt has approved more than 120 ideas, many of which have since become successful operations in one of the GE businesses. GE estimates that it is generating about US$3 billion in annual revenue from the Imagination Breakthrough portfolio of projects.

The organisation is accountable at a public level—through all the publicity they have created around their program—for implementing and funding important projects that matter, and can make at least $100 million of new money.

At a positional level, accountability lies in each internal business leader being responsible for submitting their minimum of

ORGANISATION

three proposals per year. How cool is that? Perfect use of the positional accountability currency to generate the projects that matter.

Within the Commercial Council there is peer accountability. Each of the 12 members knows there is a group phone call to participate in next month, and a meeting the month after. Nobody wants to turn up to the call or show up to the meeting not having pulled their weight. So, without even having to do anything, they hold each other to account.

The accountability around implementation needs to be about the right things. There is a danger that accountability creates fear rather than action, particularly if it is too results-focused, too early. At GE, each of the internal business leaders is accountable for coming up with three ideas: they are not accountable for coming up with three ideas that are chosen and implemented. It's the right measure to hold them accountable to—it gets them into action, but doesn't paralyse them by forcing them to come up with the perfect idea.

GE's accountability at the public level is supported by positional accountability at the internal leadership level and peer accountability at the commercial council level. It is the mix of appropriate levels of accountability that makes its public accountability a good bet.

IN SUMMARY

We saw earlier that integrity—a culture of doing what we say—is critical to the success of an organisation in implementing projects that matter. Setting the right accountability level for each project is like getting some extra insurance to make sure we fulfil our commitments. For some projects this extra insurance isn't needed, and those projects are best left at the private accountability level. In some cases, like the Atlassian hack days, peer accountability is enough. Positional accountability is very powerful as long as it is used sparingly, but don't overdo it. And, finally, for the few big, organisation-wide projects that warrant it, pull out the big guns and apply public accountability.

Three things to do

1 Pick one project that you want to have public accountability for and publicise that project.

2 Create one initiative that makes sense to operate at the private accountability level. Launch that within the organisation and see what happens.

3 Incorporate implementing projects in regular performance reviews to utilise positional accountability.

Conclusion

Man is happy only as he finds a work
worth doing—and does it well.

E. Merrill Root, educator and poet

If I rubbed the back of this book and a genie popped out and gave me three wishes for you, the reader, I would be a little surprised. But eventually I would tell the genie that my wishes for you are these.

1: You fail more

I hope that you will become great at failing; that you launch lots of ambitious projects that don't get across the line; that you have spectacular failures that you are proud of, as well as failures that are a bit embarrassing. I wish that you learn to fail without being diminished by it; that you can play full-out knowing that failing is okay; and that, of course, you are failing 50 per cent of your projects—many more failures also means many more victories.

2: You master implementation

My wish is that you build the muscle of creating and executing the projects that matter, in your life, your teams and your organisations. I wish that you recognise that implementation is the key to everything; that it doesn't come naturally; I wish that you practise it and get better at it; and that you develop an implementation mindset. More importantly, my wish is that you create the external structures, the *projects*, *framework*, *support* and *accountability*, that will turn you into an implementation ninja.

3: You get everything you want

And finally I wish that, through launching the projects that matter and mastering implementation, you achieve fulfilment and success personally, teams that are engaged and flourishing, and organisations that survive and ultimately prosper.

I would love to hear how you go. Really. Please be in touch. Send me an email at peter@petercook.com, or visit www.petercook.com and see what else I'm getting up to.

Index

Wow! You've made it to the end! Well done.

But of course this isn't the end, it's just the beginning.

There are three things to do to stay engaged.

First, there's a website full of cool resources to help you implement everything you've learned: www.newrulesofmanagement.com.

Second, visit my website, www.petercook.com and check out what else I'm up to. Sign up to get my e-newsletter, *The Word From Pete*, when you're there.

Finally, email me at peter@petercook.com. Fill me in on the projects that you are implementing, and how the book has helped. I also speak and consult about this stuff, so let me know if you want some help with it in your organisation.

Peter Cook

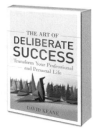

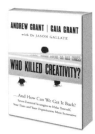